FINDING DOROTHY

Dorothy Gibson, illustrated by Harrison Fisher, 1912.

FINDING DOROTHY

A Biography of Dorothy Gibson

RANDY BRYAN BIGHAM

Edited by Jennifer Mills

Revised Edition

Lulu Press Inc | Lulu Enterprises

London   Raleigh, N.C.   Toronto

First published by Lulu Press, Inc., 2012
Revised edition released 2014
Originally published by Titanic Star, 2005

Distributed by Lulu Enterprises
Printed in the United States of America

Designed and produced by MacEvie Press Group

Lulu Press Inc
3101 Hillsboroigh St.
Raleigh, NC 27607 USA

MacEvie Press Group
3532 21st St.
San Francisco, CA 94114-3027

ISBN   978-1-105-52008-2

To Don Giovanni Barbareschi
and David and Margot Navone
with gratitude for saving Dorothy

Contents

44 pages of illustrations follow page 66

Dorothy Gibson in a 1911 Eclair Film Company publicity shot.

Prologue

THE DECK TILTING BENEATH the young woman's feet told her the ship was sinking. Leaning against the rail, she pulled her sweater closer about her as she stared into a pitch-black, frigid sky dotted with stars. The ocean below was as calm as a garden pool. Except for the slight list, the magnificent vessel seemed solid as ever. But as she gazed astern, a ghostly white mass of ice, silhouetted against heaven and sea, floated into the darkness. Slowly she turned away from the railing, realizing disaster was at hand. The deck was dim but a faint glow illuminated the shocked expression on her pale, pretty face. No one else was around. Only the shadows saw her fear.

The woman was 22-year-old actress Dorothy Gibson. She wasn't really alone but standing on a contrived set, surrounded by her director and two cameramen who were advancing slowly toward her on a rolling dais. But the terror her face registered was genuine: less than a week before this movie shoot, wearing the same sweater, Dorothy had actually survived the sinking of the *Titanic*. She was also playing to more than shadows as the cameras recorded her emotion; the film crew working with her that day admitted to being moved by the subtlety and depth of her performance. Hundreds of thousands of people, probably millions, all over the United States, Great Britain, and France would soon agree. Only one month after the real tragedy devastated the world, *Saved From the Titanic*, the first motion picture made about it, was released.

Today, the movie is lost. All that's left are four scene stills, two posters, a few advertisements, and a series of press articles and reviews that attest to a remarkable piece of filmmaking for the time, praised for its acting, advanced cinematography and special effects. The picture's value also lies in its record-breaking production, following so closely the real event it replicated. The *Titanic* was destined to sink before audiences in numerous movies, television shows, plays and musicals over the next 100 years. But the only film lost to future generations is the first phenomenal reenactment of the saga, S*aved From the Titanic*.

To cinema scholars and *Titanic* buffs the most intriguing component to this motion picture is its star, Dorothy Gibson, but little has been written of her. Who was this actress? Whatever happened to her? Legend has sprung up in the absence of fact. It is generally thought that except for her role in *Saved From the Titanic* she had done nothing noteworthy in movies. She was a mediocre talent, not even a real star, it's been claimed. Perhaps this view formed because Dorothy Gibson inexplicably disappeared from the screen after 1912. Almost no effort has been made until now to examine the scope of her acting career or the reason for her sudden retirement. The truth is, although she ended up a minor player of the silent period, Dorothy received a great deal of publicity and excellent critical reviews for the movies in which she appeared. Considered one of the most promising new actresses on her debut, her fleeting renown helped solidify the emerging "star" formula in motion pictures. What's more, the studio for which Dorothy worked was no flash in the film pan. The new American affiliate of the prestigious French-owned Éclair Company, later absorbed by Universal Pictures, was a leading producer of high-quality, one-reel dramas and comedies, crafted by some of the best directors and cinematographers from the Continent, then in the artistic vanguard of filmmaking. When Eclair started production in the United States in 1911, much was expected from the studio by the burgeoning picture industry, largely based out of the sprawling colony of Fort Lee, New Jersey. Éclair did not disappoint, becoming a training ground for important technicians of early cinema, most memorably director Maurice Tourneur.

Hired as Éclair's first American leading lady, Dorothy Gibson became noted for her work as a comedienne in a succession of popular vehicles showcasing her beauty, charm and a restrained acting style that astounded moviegoers accustomed to performers' grand theatrical gestures. Dorothy was ahead of her time in her anticipation of the soulful technique later known as "The Method;" only contemporary Mary Pickford was regarded as rivaling her in this refined approach to movie acting. The films of Dorothy Gibson proved solid money-makers. Soon one of the highest paid movie actresses, Dorothy was Éclair's hottest asset when Universal Pictures opted to buy the company's Fort Lee studios and merge their interests. The popularity of her on-screen persona and the rare skill she brought to her roles beg the conclusion that had Dorothy been more ambitious, she would have realized longer-lasting fame in the new medium.

Another half-remembered aspect of Dorothy Gibson's public life is her pre-film work as a model for one of the foremost illustrators of the day, Harrison Fisher. Whenever Dorothy is mentioned, the sobriquet of "The Harrison Fisher Girl" follows her. But as with her movie career, the extent to which she met fame as a cover model hasn't been thoroughly explored. In a way, Dorothy's stint as a muse to Fisher is more momentous than her cinematic output. Unlike her appearance in movies, of which only one is known to survive, her work for Fisher has ensured a comprehensive preservation of her image down to the present day.

Her face with its heavy-lidded eyes and wide, curling lips may be nameless, but it inspired the most prolific commercial artist of the era, whose stylized depictions of poised, healthy ingenues came to epitomize the American girl of the early 20th century. Fisher, called the "historian of American beauty," delighted in recording the feminine ideal of his time in full-color, sumptuous paintings of dainty lasses, replacing in significance his predecessor Charles Dana Gibson's pen-and-ink sketches of more sportive, tailored women. As one of Fisher's favorite models, Dorothy's youth and good looks, more recognizable to contemporaries than to modern eyes, adorned the covers of best-selling magazines like *The Saturday Evening Post, Cosmopolitan* and the *Ladies' Home Journal.* In addition, her image was reproduced on countless picture postcards, prints, posters and in Fisher's own high-priced art books.

If her professional existence has been shrouded in erroneous or fragmented data, Dorothy Gibson's private life is a greater mystery. Until recently it was believed that Dorothy, following a notorious affair with (and eventual sham marriage to) film financier Jules Brulatour, lived out her life quietly and peacefully in Paris. *Titanic* historian Phillip Gowan shattered that fiction with his astonishing discovery of Dorothy's involvement in Fascist politics and alleged espionage during the 1930s, an allegiance she renounced during World War II, only to find herself imprisoned by the Nazis in Italy as a resistance agitator. This surprising dimension to her already fascinating life has increased Dorothy's appeal beyond that of an actress or model or *Titanic* survivor to that of a deeply complex woman.

Her movements in the last decade and a half of her life remain a riddle, but enough is known to prove there was a lot more to Dorothy Gibson than beauty and talent. Her personality was a hefty mass of contradiction. Daring and confident with a warm heart and free spirit, she could be weak-willed and selfish. Savvy and highly motivated, she was also impressionable, reckless and unscrupulous. Outwardly independent and determined, the source of Dorothy's ambition was the traditionally feminine dream of marriage and family, although questionable morality was the route she chose to attain her goal. Dorothy's unorthodox values and inconsistent self-image derived partly from the influence of her permissive, seditious mother, Pauline Boesen Gibson, to whom she remained devoted, despite outrageous sympathies and predicaments which would threaten both their lives.

Dorothy Gibson's ultimate journey into disgrace and obscurity was nonetheless marked by achievement, hope, and redemption. While this book forms a long-overdue study of her career, the private story presented in these pages remains a puzzle. All the pieces of her life may never fit but a good portion of the tale has surfaced and is told, with its twists and myriad turns, in this first full-scale attempt at finding and understanding Dorothy.

Chapter 1:
Music Hath Charms
1889-1909

THE BEAUTY WHOSE FACE would one day greet millions on magazine covers and in motion pictures began her extraordinary journey amid ordinary circumstances. "I'm a daughter of Hoboken," she would one day say of her life's humble New Jersey seaport beginnings. "There is pride in that."

Pride was the order of the day for John A. Brown and his wife, the former Pauline Caroline Boesen, when they welcomed their only child, Dorothy Winifred, into their home on May 17, 1889. Although Dorothy's experiences were to carry her far from the shores of her birth, the happy little family at 320 Willow Avenue was a picture of pure Americana. The baby girl's father, of Scots descent, was an ambitious contract builder, already successful at age 24. Her mother, 23, of Danish and German extraction, was a well-educated hostess, popular among her circle of friends in the First Baptist Church of Hoboken, where the couple had been married a year and a half earlier.

Happiness was short-lived for the Browns; Dorothy was still an infant when her father died. In an age when there were few respectable careers open to women, Pauline's best chance at making ends meet for herself and her child was to remarry. Following a mourning period, during which the widow's parents, Peter and Pauline Hynsel Boesen. aided her, Pauline Brown met and wed Leonard Gibson, a prosperous Irish-born merchant. They were married in 1894, when Dorothy was almost five years old. Leonard, who adored Dorothy, adopted her. He wanted a large family but unfortunately this was not to be; Pauline gave birth twice more by 1900 but both babies died. The loss was traumatic for Pauline, and it may have shaken her faith as it was about this time that her relationship with the church — and with Leonard — began to sour.

Dorothy was fond of her stepfather but she was devoted to her mother, whose increasingly unconventional views of marriage and politics she came to share. The women had their own free-thinking ideas about religion, too, and while they kept up a façade of conservative, church-going Christianity, they became more and more secular in their mutual perspective and attitude. "My father is a great man of the spirit and is contented with the simple life," Dorothy said of Leonard many years later. "But I and my mother are bohemians and we find the pleasures of this lovely world irresistible!" In the small social orbit of Hoboken, however, the church was essential and, despite her emerging odd convictions, Pauline remained active in the local First Baptist community. Dorothy, who exhibited a musical ability at an early age, found her first chances to perform in civic, school and church plays or concerts. "It was singing that I loved," Dorothy recalled. "But I had not the slightest inkling of the stage as a profession. In those days, a girl was expected to act in amateur theatricals for charity but never was she to think of it as an occupation, and I didn't."

Little is known of Dorothy's childhood. She recalled church bazaars, trips to Atlantic City and her baptismal at age twelve as highlights of her youth. She received piano instruction and dance lessons, which, along with her natural singing talent, made her popular at parties in her teen years. But of these she related no anecdotes or special memories.

Hoboken, located on the picturesque West bank of the Hudson River, offered many amusements for the young girl and her doting mother – fairs, picnics, swimming and boating. The birthplace of baseball, the Tootsie Roll and the ice cream cone was a great place for a kid to grow up. A thriving city that was already an industrial capital in shipbuilding, Hoboken had a diverse population. An estimated 40 percent of the citizenry in the 1890s was of the immigrant class and more than half of that was German. Hoboken's Inner Harbor, or Weekawken Cove, was in fact given over to piers for steamships owned by German companies like the Hamburg-America Line. But when World War I came and the U.S. Government seized control of the docks at Hoboken, discrimination and violence against Germans was rife in the city. Pauline was shocked to see her family, friends and acquaintances ostracized, and outraged when some were sent to Ellis Island and their neighborhoods placed under martial law. Pauline's anger at the government for its ill treatment of German citizens would find a bitter outlet of expression, one none of her Hoboken church friends could ever have imagined.

As Dorothy grew into a young woman, a pretty face and graceful figure matched her beautiful voice. She had luxuriant brown hair with golden highlights, a fresh, pink complexion, and deep blue eyes. Her features were not classical but they were seductive, especially her rounded, coquettish nose and large, "kissable lips," as future patron Harrison Fisher would describe her full, expressive mouth. Liveliness and warmth added to Dorothy's allure, a magnetism that followed her throughout her life. Later commentators referred to her "delightful candor," "vitality" and "friendly sweetness." Dorothy's looks and personality didn't go unnoticed by her comparatively plain, staid mother. Pauline seems to have been enchanted by her daughter, becoming outright possessive of her. "My mother has always managed me," she admitted. "And I have always let her do it."

That Pauline was domineering is implied here. At the same time, the statement reveals Dorothy never resisted her mother's direction. Pauline's protectiveness probably arose from the loss of her other children, and as Dorothy realized that, there may never have been clashes of temperament between them. Although Pauline was later belligerent and hawkish in her dealings with almost everyone, there's no record of quarreling between mother and daughter. Surprisingly, it was only toward the end of Dorothy's fairly short life that she began to pull away from Pauline's detrimental influence.

"All her hopes and dreams centered on Dorothy who was turning out to be a very attractive young girl," observes Gibson biographer Phillip Gowan. "After moving to Manhattan, Pauline saw nothing but unlimited opportunity for her only surviving child."

The Gibson family's move to New York took place in about 1906; Dorothy remembered she was "nearly 17 (when) I stepped foot before a Broadway audience." If Dorothy's comment about never having had ambitions to go into the theatre was true, maybe it was a manifestation of Pauline's control over her daughter that permitted Dorothy's debut on the New York musical stage.

The attitude of Dorothy's father to her working in the theatre was cautiously supportive. He didn't approve of the "dissolute atmosphere" of the stage but felt that with Pauline as chaperone at rehearsals and late night shows, his stepdaughter was sufficiently protected. Leonard had good reason to be worried about Dorothy's reputation. Pauline, anxious for her daughter to "marry well," tolerated Dorothy's tendency to flirt with men and accept favors from them. She no doubt kept the truth of these courtships from Leonard. As Dorothy related:

> *The only trouble from Daddy about my venturing on the stage was my using the family name, and I honored his wishes by working for a time as Polly Stanton (sic).*

The musical Dorothy went into was an inauspicious start, being only one of a "big bunch of chorus girls in a scene of farm life and funny things." When interviewed many years on, she didn't remember much of the play, only that the production was "too wretched." The name of the show in which she first appeared has not been traced; the scene she described doesn't match programmes for any Broadway musicals from 1905-06. It's possible her debut was actually in a vaudeville song and dance act or was not in a music show at all. Whether or not her first public performance was actually on Broadway, Dorothy soon found her way to that sensational venue, appearing in a series of major musicals over the next five years. Despite the longevity of this phase of her professional life, very little has been learned about it. The only detailed personal account of her start in the entertainment world was related nearly 30 years later and it was much curtailed in favor of discussing her better remembered career as a model and movie actress.

As far as can be determined, Dorothy's first speaking part came about thanks to the gimlet eye of none other than Charles Frohman, one of the American stage's most revered producer-managers. Frohman's tasteful plays, imported adaptations of British and European successes, were equally popular stateside, both on Broadway and on the numerous road tours he arranged throughout the country. Frohman, of elfin stature and frail health, had great charm and robust style, and was the friend of many in the theatrical profession, notably Billie Burke, over whom he exercised a fatherly discipline, and Maude Adams, whom he launched in his legendary staging of *Peter Pan*. Frohman, seeing potential in Dorothy when he enticed her away from the chorus line of a musical comedy called *The Lady From Lane's* at the Lyric Theatre, put the pretty New Jersey teenager into a supporting role in his own latest musical, *The Dairymaids*. She had been appearing as "Polly Stanley" at the Lyric, as theatre researcher Victoria Alvarez has found, but Frohman must have persuaded her to start using her real name. Although her later memories imply that she used her *nom de theatre* in several productions, it's only been found in the single programme for *The Lady From Lane's.*

The Dairymaids, based on the London stage hit in which Phyllis Dare starred, had lilting music by Paul Rubens, to which Frohman added songs by another discovery of his, composer Jerome Kern. In the leading lady's role, Frohman placed Julia Sanderson. Opening at the Criterion Theatre on August 26, 1907, *The Dairymaids* endured for 86 performances, with Dorothy replacing Claudia Clarke in the credited part of the schoolgirl Rosie. Although the Internet Broadway Data Base lists Dorothy as part of the opening night cast, the programme published in the *New York Dramatic Mirror,* just following the premier, does not include her. It would seem she didn't join the Frohman play until about halfway through the show, probably late in September, just before *The Lady From Lane's* closed.

She also appeared in the chorus of *The Dairymaids* – singing, among other lyrics: "Dairymaids we, of alluring rusticity, beauties whose freshness is all unadorned." The production closed on November 16. Despite flattering appraisals of her performance ("earnest and sincere," according to the *New York Times*) and the prestige of being billed in a Frohman vehicle, Dorothy's services were not retained by the famous producer. Curiously, Dorothy didn't mention Frohman when recounting her early stage days, although his patronage provided her with the necessary cachet to proceed in her career. Why was she released from her contract? Is it possible Dorothy had already begun her dalliances with men, and that Frohman, a stickler for the morals of his female stars, discharged her for perceived indecencies?

Dorothy soon found regular work in musicals through the agency of the Shubert Brothers (J.J. and Lee) who ran the biggest production and management combine in the American theatre at the time. Famous for their fabulous revues with huge casts and risque subjects, the Shubert Brothers were leading political players in the unfolding of a free market in the business, opposing the creative and financial monopoly imposed by the Theatrical Syndicate. They are said to have offered the highest pay to performers and, unlike Frohman, didn't care about the cavorting of their actresses, which was reportedly legion. Dorothy did not elaborate on her new contract when discussing her career in later years but it appears it was a non-exclusive deal that allowed her to appear independently without compromising her standing as a Shubert performer. A surviving 1907 ledger recording her salary (a respectable $53 a week) does not refer to her duties. Dorothy took advantage of the opportunity to work elsewhere, sporadically joining a number of touring companies along the East Coast and in Canada over the next three years. Some of these shows appear to have overlapped her appearances in Shubert productions, indicating she was managing a busy performing schedule. Among the traveling productions she appeared in were T*he Alter of Friendship* (1907) and *The Mayor and the Manicure* (1908), which she joined again on the road in 1909. In the latter incarnation she received good notices for her ingénue role as Ruth Foster, including praise in the *New York Dramatic Mirror* which found her "exhilaratingly exuberant and so truly girlish that at times it seemed she was merely playing herself."

Although press releases during her later film career would refer to her having first "gained some attention on the stage," there's no documentation that Dorothy had major speaking parts in shows other than *The Dairymaids* and *The Mayor and the Manicure.* Yet good looks went a long way on the Great White Way, and future directors engaged her regularly for her attractiveness, graceful carriage and singing ability. Nevertheless, she remained either a chorine or minor player in the shows for which she was hired thereafter.

Her appearance in Shubert productions, mainly those staged at the enormous, 5,000-seat Hippodrome Theatre, soon brought her a foretaste of celebrity as one of "Stageland's most beautiful girls." According to one contemporary critic, Dorothy regarded her looks

> *as not merely a medium to arouse envy in others of her sex but as a gift from her Creator, by the grace of which she earns an honest living.*

The first really successful show in which she appeared was *Sporting Days.* Opening September 5, 1908 and enduring for a solid eight months, *Sporting Days* cast 500 dancers, singers and extras in such gargantuan scenes as a baseball field and stadium. In this scene Dorothy was one of a chorus of lovely lasses representing spectators in the stands, each in white frocks and flower-decked hats. *Sporting Days*, actually comprising three shows, was billed as "A Triple Bill of Melodrama, Ballet and Spectacle." "It was a hit and quite thrilling," Dorothy said. "All the Shubert shows were romantic extravagances. Everyone went to them."

Theatre Magazine for October 1908 considered the production "superb" and a "triumph," commenting that its beauty "has rarely been equaled." The reviewer was particularly fond of the finale, a scene called the "Golden Garden," which was judged a

> *splendid pageant, the most striking feature being a tableau where the gowns worn by the chorus form the American flag which, when illuminated, appears to be waving.*

The critique concluded that with *Sporting Days* the Shuberts "certainly have gone one better in their already lengthy list of wonderful Hippodrome shows." After the play closed in May 1909, Dorothy rested a month or so before beginning rehearsals for the next lavish Hippodrome show, *A Trip to Japan,* in which she was again part of a chorus of tremendous size. She would follow this with yet another choral role in the latest Shubert fantasy, 1910's *The International Cup.* But Dorothy still had no exclusive contract with the Shuberts and so was free to join a tour of the Metropolitan Comic Opera Company in the summer of that year, appearing in Boston and Philadelphia.

As a "Hippodrome Girl" Dorothy worked hard. According to Broadway historian Robert Baral, the Hippodrome offered actors the steadiest work in New York, the theatre being open 40 weeks a season. With two performances daily, Dorothy and her fellow cast members played to an average of 12,000 people each day. Dorothy dismissed her time as a showgirl as requiring "nothing special." A glimpse of her sense of humor is caught in her disarming statement that

> *all we did was stand around in pretty hats, lean on our parasols, and purr through*

a few ditties. It was easy to get into a Shubert show. The casts were so big, anybody could get in. I think my aunt was in one.

A Trip to Japan ran for a whopping 447 performances and *The International Cup* for 333 shows. It was during the run of the former production that Dorothy's life would change – literally overnight – when she was spotted from the audience by the man who would jump-start her path to fame.

Chapter 2:
The Pink of Perfection
1909-1911

SHOWGIRLS DIDN'T WANT for male attention. The Victorian and Edwardian period was the heyday of the stage door Johnny. Actresses' dressing rooms on Broadway were aflutter with flowers, chocolates and gifts of jewelry, often sent by the richest men in the world. Back-stage corridors teemed with the distinguished admirers themselves, each patiently awaiting an introduction to the object of their desire. Dorothy had her share of top-hatted, monocle-wearing visitors but none was as welcomed as the handsome young man who presented himself to her in the autumn of 1909.

Thirty-one-year-old bachelor Harrison Fisher had with him no presents or flowers when a Hippodrome Theatre maid swung open the door to the dressing room belonging to the chorus line and directed him to "a slip of a thing chirping on a stool at a mirror, sur-rounded by her friends." As the preeminent commercial artist of his day – pursued by doe-eyed girls (and their match-making mothers) as much as he was hounded by reporters – the gift he had to offer Dorothy that evening was more valuable than any bauble he could have bestowed. Dorothy recounted in a Sunday supplement to the *New York American:*

> *Mr. Fisher was wonderful, the way he entered, very gentlemanly, but very busi-ness-like. He did not kiss my hand. He shook it. He told me his name but it did not strike me at first. He said, 'Miss Gibson, I admire your face. May I paint it?' I laughed until I realized he was in earnest. And then it dawned on me that here was the Harrison Fisher offering to engage me as a model! I went white and all the girls around me squealed."*

Fisher's impression of Dorothy was that she was "marvelously modest," "highly individual in her taste," and "brimming with girlish, friendly sweetness." Although there are alternate stories of Dorothy's first meeting with Harrison Fisher, Dorothy's account is the least dra-matic and therefore, the most plausible. One account claimed that the great artist was so smitten that he

> *went down on his knees and begged the lovely Miss Dorothy to come away to his studio so that he might at once commit to canvas her gorgeous features, glorious curves and glamorous youth. She consented and resigned her post on the spot to become Mr. Fisher's latest muse.*

11

THE PINK OF PERFECTION

Dorothy probably did begin working for Fisher very soon afterwards but she didn't leave her stage work. Instead, she supplemented her earnings from Shubert shows with her pay from Fisher, which ranged from $15 to $40 a sitting, according to estimates given by other Fisher models from this period. Dorothy recognized the importance of her new job but she downplayed it. As she said in a 1930s interview:

> *I was fortunate to be discovered, in a manner of speaking, by Mr. Fisher. But he had many models, and some of them were far prettier than I was. I do not know what he saw in me. Youthful charm I may have had but I never thought I was a great beauty.*

Fisher may not have found her to be a great beauty either. He seldom proclaimed any of his models to be perfectly beautiful. Fisher explained in one interview that

> *models are hard to find, for nine out of ten of them lack beauty, and their faces, if faithfully reproduced by the painter, would be dull, flat and unattractive. No matter how near perfect a girl's features, figure and complexion may be, the quality that makes her beautiful lies beneath them and uses them only as a mirror with which to reflect her charm.*

He went on to say that "character, innate refinement and beauty of mind" were what he sought in models and that only the American girl fit his ideal. "I could not find in Europe a single model that my American public would accept," he said. And therein lay Harrison Fisher's peculiar fame.

Supplanting Charles Dana Gibson, whose sketches interpreted the mature beauty of his wife and muse, the former Irene Langhorne, Fisher with his pastel depictions of younger, daintier women was enjoying by 1909 an immense vogue as the "greatest portrayer of American womanhood," according to *Harper's Bazaar.* One advertisement for his work called him "the kingpin in the art alley of America."

Working mainly in the mediums of crayon, oils and watercolor, Brooklyn-born, California-bred Fisher was already commanding an annual salary of $60,000 when he met Dorothy, his "girlie pictures" having graced the covers of all the nation's top magazines as well as the pages of a series of best-selling novels. Each portrait going for as much as $800 plus royalties, Fisher's lovelies were seen in picture postcards, calendars, theatrical programmes and posters, sheet music, greeting cards and all manner of merchandise, from candy boxes and cookie tins to glassware and dishes. Meantime, publications like the *Ladies Home Journal* and *Cosmopolitan* boosted subscriptions by offering readers selections of full-color lithographs of his work for framing. These reprints sold in the millions, ranging in price from 15 cents a picture to a choice of a dozen for $1.50.

Cosmopolitan, which did the biggest business in selling Fisher prints, was the magazine with which he would become most identified. While the *Saturday Evening Post,* with its enormous weekly circulation of 1,250,000 copies, launched Fisher on a national scale, *Cosmopolitan* came to avidly embrace his work. The magazine's high quality color printing revealed his painted ladies to best effect and because of that (and its reputation for guaranteeing premium prices for illustrations) Fisher was loyal to *Cosmopolitan* for the rest of his career. In fact, from 1912 until his death in 1934, nearly every issue of *Cosmopolitan* featured a Fisher image on the front, earning him the reputation of "king of the magazine cover," as his competitor and friend Howard Chandler Christy once referred to him.

Fisher had also illustrated a succession of well-received books of his own ¬¬-- deluxe albums of poetry and short stories, published by Scribner's, Bobbs-Merrill and Dodd-Mead. Several of these books, particularly *A Dream of Fair Women* and *Bachelor Belles* went into numerous reissues. Fisher's prolific output brought him tremendous acclaim, much of it unwanted by the quiet artist. Nevertheless, in a contemporary profile, *Cosmopolitan* wrote that

> *At the top of the heap stands Harrison Fisher, creator of the Fisher Girl, and most popular of all Americans who ply brush and pencil for reproduction. By reason of his industry and because of the uniform soundness of his drawings and color sense, he is the acknowledged master of the pretty girl picture.*

Another article claimed "he was one of the first to see that the New World had produced a type of woman with the characteristic 'look of race.'" Moreover, the press claimed that as the "real depicter of the healthy, well-poised, clear-eyed girl," Fisher had "neither peer nor superior." He was even called the "historian of American beauty," painting the modern girl just "as she is, bouyant and carefree."

While the media of that day trumpeted Fisher's evocation of femininity as epitomizing the contemporary American girl, the truth is he was only idealizing a type that was already nationally admired. His girls therefore represented the American "dream" of beauty rather than its reality. Journalist Barbara Andrews wrote that Fisher's "drawings were romantic, focusing on the fantasies of the nation's women, on what women wanted to be, not what they were." He did, however, make periodic departures in his depictions of women, painting less typical beauties. He had grown tired, so he admitted, of drawing "goo-goo eyes and fluffy hair and little noses and pouty lips."

It was likely his quest for uncommon beauty that attracted Harrison Fisher to Dorothy Gibson's exotic Germanic looks. What her features lacked in perfection, they made up for in the characteristics he felt she had in abundance – "femininity, grace, personality and intelligence," traits he identified as elemental to true beauty. Another requirement for achieving great beauty in Fisher's opinion was a finely-honed fashion sense. In an article he wrote for *Dress Magazine*, he lectured on the essentials of correct clothing:

> *Externals do count, however broad we may think our views to be.... To be unkempt is the unpardonable sin.... The consciousness of dress deficiencies – an ill-fitting frock, shabby gloves and shoes, a disorderly or careless adjustment of garments – can outdistance the nimblest wit and swamp the best-equipped conversational wit.*

THE PINK OF PERFECTION

Fisher admitted that as an illustrator he was trained "far beyond the average in the intricacies of woman's dress" because "any detail out of character remains to mock its creator."

As Dorothy's actual features differ only slightly from Fisher's romanticized interpretation of them, it's fairly easy to pick her out among the artist's many models, all of whom were distinctly different in type and coloring. The verification of images of Dorothy among Fisher's body of work is an arbitrary task and therefore not infallible. Still, more than a dozen portraits bearing a strong resemblance to photographs of her have been identified. Fisher realized the flaws in Gibson's facial structure (very round eyes and a longish nose with bulbous tip) and posed her to best advantage for the illusion of greater beauty. He generally painted her with her head elevated, so as to soften the length of her nose, and with her eyes lowered so that they appeared half-closed. A sultry countenance was the effect produced, although if one regards these images less sentimentally, one imagines Dorothy was always peering over something that obstructed her view. This technique wasn't effortless on the part of the model. "A thing I hated was keeping my head raised for an hour or more," Dorothy said. "I believe I have a permanent crick in my neck from the strain."

Yet the dramatically raised mandible or jaw line that was a trademark of Fisher's portrayal of women in profile was utilized in only a few of his paintings of Dorothy; he preferred to capture her face-on with her head slightly angled. Several pictures also show her face lowered so as to give the full effect of her large eyes. In these, Fisher tended to reduce the size of her nose, although its shape is always accurately drawn. As another leading Fisher model, Margery Allwork, would claim, he also had a propensity for augmenting his models' breasts and altering their hair color to suit him. Allwork, who was fair-headed, sometimes appeared raven-haired. Likewise, Dorothy, a light brunette, was depicted often as a blonde.

Perhaps the most striking in the iconography that has been established of Dorothy in the Fisher *oeuvre*, is the image entitled "Roses." In this picture, one of Fisher's few full-length studies of Dorothy, he portrays her in characteristic pose, her head raised challengingly, the faintest of smiles on her face. Perched on a delicately brocaded gilt chair, one hand clasping a long-stemmed rose and the other resting on her hip, she wears a "gala supper gown of undulating pink silk" with an empire waist and long train. On her waves of pale brown hair rests a huge black "Merry Widow" hat with gray plumes, tipped to one side in the latest Parisian *geste*. She seems to be staring into the distance, perhaps searching out her escort in the crowd at a restaurant. This portrait, one of the earliest identifiable Dorothy Gibson images by Harrison Fisher, appeared on postcards and in several of Fisher's books. A 1909 newspaper story about Fisher and his models included "Roses" as an illustration with the equally roseate caption: "Mr. Fisher's newest discovery is Miss Dorothy Gibson, who shares her beauty with the sweetest of flowers."

A similar Fisher portrait from this time whose likeness is attributed to Dorothy is called "My Queen." It was chosen as the frontispiece for Fisher's 1910 album, *A Garden of Girls*. Again seated at some fashionable function, probably an opera, Dorothy wears a lustrous, trailing black dress topped by an ermine-edged, pale turquoise cape. On her head sits another giant, feather-laded black hat with a cocked brim. One of her arms is extended, its talons clutching a lorgnette. Her face is inclined as usual but there is a broader smile this time, and she's looking directly ahead, as if to exclaim, "There you are!"

FINDING DOROTHY

A third Dorothy picture, called "Music Hath Charms," borrowing boldly from Shakespeare, is the only one Dorothy recalled by name. It may also be the most significant portrait for which she posed.

> *It is my favorite of the pictures I sat to. Mr. Fisher gave me the original and I have kept it ever since and treasure it. I have even made a keepsake of the hat I wore in it. The piano in that picture was Mr. Fisher's own.*

In "Music Hath Charms," a love-sick Dorothy leans upon a piano and gazes into the eyes of a sleek young man who is playing and singing to her. Fisher has drawn her in complete profile, her mass of soft tresses tucked under a white picture hat trimmed with peach ribbon. She wears a white eyelet lace tunic, ornamented with twin black bows, and a white cloth, box-pleated walking skirt, under the hem of which is glimpsed the dainty toe of a white leather boot. In a romantic gesture common in Fisher's paintings, he has depicted Dorothy as having removed one of her long kid gloves; it's held in her gloved hand along with a matching white parasol, striped in black and peach. "Music Hath Charms" was also used as cover art for *The Butterfly Man*, a novel by George Barr McCutcheon, published in 1910. Several other Fisher pictures of Dorothy appeared in McCutcheon's *What's His Name,* released the following year.

Exciting as it was for Dorothy to pose for Fisher, and as pleased as he appears to have been with her, their association was unaccountably interrupted. The break seems to have happened after Dorothy had been sitting for Fisher for about two months. Was it the exigencies of her simultaneous performing career with the Shubert Brothers that caused her to leave Fisher's studio? Or had there been some personal entanglement between the two? The latter seems possible. During the winter of 1909 Dorothy had fallen in love with George Henry Battier, Jr., a young pharmacist. Had Fisher chronicled this courtship — or possibly his personal infatuation with Dorothy — in the idyllic "Music Hath Charms?" If that picture was meant as a tribute to Fisher's own love for her, it could explain why he allegedly gave Dorothy the original and why she always prized it.

Battier, originally from Memphis, Tennessee, probably began his involvement with Dorothy as one of her backstage suitors at the Hippodrome. Enthralled by his showgirl sweetheart, he may have been jealous and possessive of her, especially after she began posing for Harrison Fisher. Did Battier suspect his girlfriend was having a fling with the famous illustrator? There's no way to be certain, but the rumor of an amour persists among Fisher aficionados today. It also would be in keeping with Dorothy's lifelong penchant for promiscuous affairs. At any rate, there's no definite proof of a romance, only gossip. Whatever else did or didn't take place, immediately after quitting work as a model for Fisher, Dorothy accepted Battier's proposal of marriage. They were wed on February 10, 1910 and set up household together in Manhattan.

"The union lasted only a few months," wrote Gibson expert Phillip Gowan in his 2002 study. "By summer they had separated, and Dorothy was once again living with her mother and stepfather. That would not be the end of her romantic life — or her marital woes."

THE PINK OF PERFECTION

Neither would it be the end of her involvement with Fisher. During the run of *The International Cup*, late in 1910, Dorothy resumed modeling for him. She gave no reason for showing back up at his West 37th Street studio, but she was obviously welcomed, to judge by the ensuing stream of cameo portraits of her, three of which are the most faithful renditions of Dorothy that Fisher ever drew. After her Hippodrome engagement wrapped up in March of the following year, Dorothy began working full time for Fisher. If an affair had sprung from their earlier working relationship, by now the attraction had dulled, as Dorothy's words indicate:

> *Mr. Fisher was odd. He was very meticulous. And he was not much for small talk. He was kind most of the time, pleasant and considerate, but he was also prone to foul moods…. He could not abide being interrupted in his work and permitted no criticism whatsoever…. His was the last word absolutely.*

During this phase of Dorothy's sitting for Fisher, the trio of cameos that would eventually earn for her the title of "The Original Harrison Fisher Girl," were enchantingly intimate representations.

The first became known as "Mary," the name given its postcard incarnation. But it initially appeared untitled as the cover for the *Saturday Evening Post*'s April 8, 1911 issue. The likeness, also seen in a print included in Fisher's book *American Belles* (published later that year), is radiant in its delicate rendering of her opalescent complexion, deep blue eyes, gracefully arching brows, wavy hair and full, red lips with their dimpled edges. Fisher ensured the impact of Dorothy's fine coloring by framing it in the stark black and white tones of her veiled, feathered hat and bow-trimmed blouse. The image is exquisite in its treatment of detail and texture but there is something more that draws the viewer. There is a bewitching nonchalance in Dorothy's expression. Neither the magazine cover nor postcard versions of this cameo capture her enticing moodiness as does the crisp lithographic copy (utilizing the new four-color process) that appeared in *American Belles*.

A second picture that helped secure Dorothy's acclaim as Fisher's "favorite model" and "regular muse," was also published in *American Belles*. It too is known by its whimsical postcard title – "Refreshments" – and saw its widest circulation as cover art, appearing as the face of *Cosmopolitan*'s June 1911 edition. Today Fisher collectors covet this picture, which shows Dorothy's face lowered over the tall glass of lemonade she's sipping through a soda straw. Although she has been painted as a blonde, Dorothy's features, especially her big blue eyes, are unmistakable under the black hat she wears with its pink satin bow and turquoise pin. The wrinkling under her eyes has been softened and her somewhat flaring nostrils have been scaled down, but Dorothy's essential charm and allure is faithfully preserved.

Conscious always of fashion, Fisher has drawn her in a white gauzy blouse, gathered at the neck, a turquoise ring and gold bangle bracelet. Her expression seems pensive and shy at first glance but a closer look reveals greater intensity in the eyes, as though she's gazing longingly at some beau across a soda fountain counter. Dorothy autographed a copy of "Refreshments" for columnist Adela Rogers St. Johns when she met her for an interview some time later. "I was drinking sarsaparilla, not lemonade," she said when St. Johns showed the print to her. "But it brings back memories of my girlhood. I was just a child then and frightened of everything." Actually, Dorothy was at least 21 years old when she posed for the picture and, if it's a true reflection of her mood, she was far from shy.

The third in the series of famous pictures of Dorothy that Fisher completed soon after her return to his studio, is again one included in his *American Belles* (out of 16 tipped-in prints, she is the subject of at least six). Called "Bows Attract Beaus" in the inevitable postcard edition, it was selected for the July 1911 cover of *Cosmopolitan*. As in the picture "Mary," the effect of Dorothy's rosy skin and fluffy light hair in "Bows Attract Beaus" is highlighted by the neutral shades of gray, black and white which Fisher has used for her blouse and plumed Napoleonic hat, tied in a loose bow under her chin. Also like "Mary" and "Refreshments," this picture is remarkable as much for its evocation of the spirit of the sitter, as for the beauty of the illustrator's technique. Fisher is telling a story with his brush. In "Bows Attract Beaus," there is none of the limpid innocence of some of his other models; there's a knowingness in Dorothy's eyes. She seems to be peeking out of a window in observance of some secret scene. The suggestion may be close to the truth, as Dorothy was certainly privy to the inside scoop on the media hoopla swirling around her employer at the time.

Labeled the "models' war" by the *New York Herald*, the situation found Fisher walking the tight rope of public opinion. Fisher could not have expected the intense reaction from the press to the decision he made at the conclusion of his much-touted "quest for the ideal model," a campaign blitz concocted by the artist that obviously went awry. Fisher, who commuted between his Manhattan studio and his house in San Francisco, had discovered while on a visit home an attractive young lady named Rita Maurine Rasmussen (later Mrs. Fred Montague), whom the *New York Times* heralded as possessing "a new type of beauty" in a January 1911 editorial. Tina Skinner wrote in her biography of Fisher that such an assertion was enough to set off a heated debate:

> Other newspapers helped stoke a growing fire of envy, and sniping between the coasts ensued over the virtue of resident women. Now the pride of California, Rasmussen was celebrated in West Coast and Midwest newspapers while New York women were slurred.

Fisher, who employed the majority of his models in New York, didn't help his case when he began to trumpet the beauty and charm of Rasmussen – "The Girl of the Golden West" he called her. At least he didn't criticize his East Coast camp of beauties – hard workers like Jeanne Robert Foster (his first muse in 1903), Margery Allwork, Irene Howley and Dorothy Gibson. But Rasmussen did point a scornful finger, which is what sparked the furor. On her arrival in New York to begin modeling for Fisher, she gave a round of ill-advised interviews, in which she referred derisively to her fellow models – and all "Northern women" – as looking grave and unapproachable. "New York girls look as if there was a $5 fine for smiling," she told reporters. "There's no use looking like a plaster cast."

Letters of indignation poured into newspapers and Fisher's studio. Meantime, one of his top models, Lucy Cotton, resigned in angry protest to Fisher's indulgence of Rasmussen. She was so mad, following a fight with Fisher, she went directly to work for the artist's competitor, Howard Chandler Christy. Another of Fisher's models, Katherine "Kitty" Clements, who served as his secretary and later became his lover, did her best to allay the discontent among his fans and corps of regular sitters, not least of whom was Dorothy. From what can be learned of her involvement in this debacle, Dorothy kept her cool and waited the storm out, expressing in interviews only her "respect and faithfulness" to Fisher. If she was hurt by his tolerance of Rasmussen's antics, she didn't admit it. Dorothy seems to have genuinely taken it all in her stride. For instance, she claimed Fisher told her a "favorite caprice" of his while painting was to blend her features with Rasmussen's to "make the perfect girl." Perhaps he was only flattering her. Even so, Dorothy said he had a habit

> of using Miss Rasman's (sic) brows and nose with my eyes and mouth. Mr. Fisher told me I had very kissable lips and that they were my prettiest feature…. The first picture I recall seeing my features mixed up with hers in was one where I was in furs with a pug dog to my chin.

Throughout the controversy, Dorothy joined her voice of understanding with that of another Fisher model, Mary Elizabeth Forbes, who told a columnist for the *New York Courier* that "real beauty is universal, after all. It knows no geographic boundaries."

Asked by entertainment writer Roberta Courtlandt how she defined beauty and if she felt "rivaled" by Rasmussen, Dorothy cautiously replied that she believed in "the beauty of the soul and of congeniality," and that she did "not wish to be in competition with anyone." Her decision to steer clear of the backbiting actually fueled her popularity with the New York dailies which were soon referring to her as "Fisher's perfect muse" and ultimately, as the *New York Times* would persist in calling her, "The Original Harrison Fisher Girl." This nickname, once thought to have designated Dorothy as one of the illustrator's first models, pertained rather to her having "all the qualities of the beauties in his original drawings."

The tagline seemed fitting and soon caught on in the press, Dorothy having posed, so the *Dramatic Mirror* would claim, "for much of (Fisher's) better work." As the moniker was repeated in articles about Dorothy, she soon adopted it as her own. One can imagine this didn't thrill her rival, Rita Rasmussen, who soon quit modeling for Fisher following an alleged dispute with the artist – and with Kitty Clements, of whom she was likely jealous. But did Rasmussen also resent the press' adulation of Dorothy? It may have rankled with her; during a public appearance in 1934 she claimed it was she who was "The Original Harrison Fisher Girl."

The "war of the models" may have begun with bitterness over Rita Rasmussen's ascendance to fame but it ended in solidarity after her departure, Dorothy becoming the media's odd's-on favorite among Fisher's bevy of girls. Even well into the next year, after she had exchanged full-time modeling for film acting, Dorothy remained, as the *New York Daily Telegraph* claimed, "'the beautiful 'Harrison Fisher Girl,' still celebrated "from coast to coast."

Lovely as Dorothy was and as well-received as Fisher's pictures of her were, more publicity probably ought to have gone to Margery Allwork, who was the painter's most loyal model by far, working for him for over twenty years, from 1906 until 1927. Her elegant, ageless face, with its signature tipped-up nose and small lips, can be seen more frequently than that of any other model throughout Fisher's extensive body of work. Of the illustrator's known sitters, if there was one who could truly be called "The Original Harrison Fisher Girl," it was Margery Allwork.

Today, Dorothy Gibson's face still peeps out at connoisseurs of vintage magazines, postcards, posters, calendars and other paper collectibles. Few know her name but all are captivated by her sometimes wistful, sometimes naughty, but always confident expression. In a few short months Dorothy, through the brushstrokes of a genius, came to personify the American Girl in her every mood and activity — dancing, driving cars, walking dogs, rowing canoes, sipping cold drinks, reading poetry, singing songs, being courted, getting married. These last scenarios were sore spots for Dorothy: contrary to the contentment indicated in her portraits, the Harrison Fisher Girl was dissatisfied with her life. Tired of seeing herself in the raptures of love on a magazine cover, she wanted the private happiness her painted likeness was enjoying. Her failed marriage had left her yearning again for a man to adore. Modeling was also, she said, "a terrific bore," and she welcomed a new adventure. Soon, Dorothy would get her man and more adventure than she could handle.

Chapter 3:
My Queen
1911

AN ENTIRELY NEW CAREER, and a life to go with it, opened up for Dorothy Gibson in early 1911. Separated from George Battier, Dorothy was living with her parents. Pauline had grown increasingly distant from Leonard and his religious views, but she remained active in church for the social outlet it offered her as well as the possibility it provided of snagging a rich husband for her daughter. Dorothy's beauty and sudden celebrity as a Harrison Fisher model was enough to attract attention anywhere, but by the time she turned 22 years old that May, the seemingly demure miss who sat in Sunday services with her mother had another claim to fame. She had become an actress in the budding entertainment field of the motion picture.

1911 was a turning point in the medium of film. The age of the nickelodeon, with its audiences of poor immigrants and rowdy neighborhood kids, was giving way to a larger, more sophisticated market. The novelty of the moving image was no longer an entry in a raree show but was rapidly pulling in men and women of every class and background. The new theatres reflected the change in class of their patrons. By the end of 1911, corner nickelodeons were being replaced by elegant movie houses, modeled after Paris' magnificent 3,500-seat Gaumont Palace, which had opened amid great fanfare earlier that year. The genre had already attracted as directors and cinematographers some of the most gifted artists and craftsmen in the world. Meanwhile, actors from the "legitimate" stage, who for a decade had regarded movie performers as menials, were being tempted into the arena by contracts with fantastic salaries. Even classical French tragediennes Sarah Bernhardt, Gabrielle Rejane and Cecile Sorel ventured into films in 1911. Bernhardt, in particular, was enthusiastic about the future of moviemaking. Starring in the acclaimed French-American production of *Camille,* she said in a press release that she had "conquered a new medium," adding that she "never thought I would be a film, but now that I am two whole reels of pictures, I rely for my immortality upon these records."

Dorothy was entering film at a propitious moment in its financial and commercial evolution. In a special issue devoted to the motion picture industry, *Billboard* magazine, the first mainstream amusement journal to recognize the power of the cinema, estimated that the more than 20,000 movie houses across the United States were bringing in an annual revenue of $240 million. With the popularity of the new entertainment, a higher quality was demanded by patrons whose monetary support, in turn, enabled producers to meet that demand with more expensive and artistic vehicles. As *Billboard* expounded:

> *During no period since its inception has the motion picture business made such extraordinary strides in one peculiar phase of it than it has during the past year. This is in the way of an increase in the merit of pictures, both from the standpoint of subject and execution. A year ago, even those who were in close touch with the situation would scarcely have forecast the degree of improvement that has been effected.*

Billboard further noted that as the industry was becoming "more highly systemized every day," it was offering a better product in film direction, acting, photography, distribution, sales and exhibition. Technological advancements were being made, too. One-reel pictures of 10-15 minutes were still the standard vehicle, but longer "feature films" of two to five reels were already appearing. Even color films had arrived as had movies equipped with an experimental mechanism for sound. Dorothy was also coming into the movies at a time of transformation in the marketing of screen performers themselves. Today the Hollywood formula of publicizing actors is taken for granted, long since accepted as an invaluable tool for promoting individual films and the industry as a whole. But in 1911, this system had just begun. Producers were realizing that audiences wanted to know the names of their stock players and that these anonymous "silver sheet figures" could be as profitable drawing cards as any Broadway or vaudeville personality. As one movie fan wrote to the *New York Dramatic Mirror* that year:

> *We like to know who's who, just as we do when we go to the legitimate theatres and pick up a programme to follow the players.*

Even so, some filmmakers, notably Biograph Studios, one of the more prolific early production companies, resisted the "star" method outright for fear of the inevitable hike in players' salaries. It was producer and distributor Carl Laemmle, head of the Independent Motion Picture Company (IMP) and future founder of Universal Studios, who marketed the first bona fide "movie star" in 1910. As a publicity stunt to outwit competitors, Laemmle acquired the Biograph leading lady, Florence Lawrence, promising her more money along with the unprecedented promotion of her own name in connection with the pictures in which she was featured.

Lawrence's publicity campaign was a success and rival filmmakers, like Vitagraph and Kalem studios, followed suit, advertising (in print and on screen) the names of already familiar faces – and new ones – in hopes of pleasing fans. Apart from Florence Lawrence, the first brace of American film idols included favorites like Western hero "Broncho Billy" Anderson, oversized comedian John Bunny, dapper romantic leads Francis X. Bushman and Maurice Costello, and high-spirited ingenue Mabel Normand.

MY QUEEN

Dorothy Gibson would soon join this first generation of silver screen royalty, her beauty, charm and talent winning for her a movie presence that, while short-lived, was as sharply defined as those of her contemporaries. It was Laemmle, in fact, who gave Dorothy her first chance as a "likely photoplay heroine." Unfortunately, his director, Thomas Ince, was less smitten. "Hired on the spot by Mr. Laemmle," as Dorothy blithely recounted, she was ordered to report for work at the IMP studios at Fort Lee, the New Jersey hamlet that had become America's picture-making capital. But once there, she "was used only as an extra and in a few supporting roles," according to journalist Adela Rogers St. Johns. Laemmle, whom Dorothy remembered as "a jolly fellow when he wasn't snapping at you," promptly forgot all about her, or so she believed, leaving her to "disappear into the background on the set and off."

Dorothy was in an undetermined number of films while at IMP, although a profile of her in the *Dramatic Mirror* intimated she had many roles while there and that she appeared "with success" in them. If so, they made no impression on her. She did remember that one of her first pictures was a comedy starring Florence Lawrence. In it Dorothy was cast as a chorine, which she laughingly confessed "was not very hard to play." The film's title isn't known but it was probably *A Show Girl's Strategem*, released February 13, 1911. It's possible Dorothy also appeared in films with Mary Pickford, who was an IMP stock player during this period.

Although Fort Lee and Laemmle would later figure more prominently in her life, by April Dorothy had set her sights on a better position with the larger and more prosperous Lubin Studios, based in Philadelphia and run by America's first big-time movie magnate, Siegmund Lubin. The Lubin company was one to reckon with in the early days of cinema. It was pioneering in that it operated studios across the country, not just on the East Coast, while most production companies were content to send out units whenever location filming was necessary. In addition, Siegmund Lubin owned a national chain of theatres and manufactured his own cameras and projectors. When Dorothy showed up at the brand-new Lubin plant in Philadelphia, located at 20th Street and Indiana Avenue, she was awe-struck by the million-dollar complex, complete with electrically lit stages big enough for making several films at one time. This commune, perhaps rivaling that of Fort Lee in size and artistic output, was known as "Lubinville." Dorothy was hired by the Lubin company as a member of its main stock company and given bigger, though still supporting, roles. Lubin's reputation for the technical excellence of its films had attracted a loyal corps of actors, two of whom would go on to become influential directors – Frank Borzage and Henry King.

One of Dorothy's Lubin co-stars, herself still a struggling starlet, was Pearl White, the future heroine of the legendary adventure serial, *The Perils of Pauline*. Dorothy appeared in at least one picture with White, again unidentified by title, in which they portrayed "sad little waifs." This was most likely *Angel of the Slums*, released May 15. The two aspiring leading ladies would remain friends for many years. "Pearl is my idea of a class-act," Dorothy said in 1924, after both had retired from movie-making. "She's the best." Neither Pearl White nor Dorothy made great strides at Lubin and both began searching elsewhere for better parts and higher pay. Dorothy was also looking for a little respect; a fellow stock player with the same last name was being confused with her and receiving credit in the press for Lubin films that actually featured Dorothy. In two instances, *Motion Picture Story*

Magazine cleared the air, confirming that it was Dorothy Gibson, not Frances Gibson, who appeared in *Good for Evil* and *The Senorita's Conquest.*

Continuing to pose for Harrison Fisher and enjoying the celebrity that came with the honor, Dorothy wondered why she was stuck with less than plum roles in the movies. Her face on the covers of the *Ladies' Home Journal* in February and the *Saturday Evening Post* that April had brought a flurry of news articles about her, and it was that attention that must have won her the job at Lubin. Yet directors seemed content to use her as a piece of pretty scenery. Her fame as a model attracted the studios to her but once she was signed she fell inexplicably through the cracks. Commenting years afterward, Dorothy believed she was denied better material at IMP and Lubin because she didn't "emote," the screen-acting term pervasive at the time. As Dorothy said:

> In those days actors were very demonstrative and ran around the stage like a twister. I never had the energy to do that. The cameras did not catch anything, the people at Lubin told me. I was all wood and lacking in spirit, they said, which kept me in bit parts.

The melodramatic technique of her acting contemporaries – wide eyes, raised brows, flailing hands – was considered an essential approach by directors of the silent era, including D.W. Griffith in his formative years. Likewise, Herbert Brenon's definition of movie acting was "stage technique emphasized and enlarged." But Dorothy's style, which she seems to have unconsciously developed, was more naturalistic, exhibiting a restraint and subtlety not yet fully appreciated. Of the female stars of her day, only Mary Pickford and Alice Joyce would become noted for delivering performances with the same understated realism for which Dorothy was adept. It wasn't long before she had the opportunity to reveal her abilities as a leading lady to the movie-loving American public but the opportunity would come from a foreign film company.

Paris-based Les Societe Francaise des Films et Cinematographes Éclair, commonly known as Éclair, was one of the top producers of motion pictures in Europe at a time when the Continent was the indisputable artistic and technological leader in the industry. Together with fellow French cinema giants Pathe Freres, Gaumont, Melies and Lumiere, Éclair set a high example of excellence in many commercial aspects of the business while its assemblage of directors, photographers and actors were widely considered to be among the most distinguished in the world.

Éclair, initially recognized for its stylish comedies and historical dramas, had since become celebrated for the episodic or "chapter play" format in films, first experienced by moviegoers in the sensational *Nick Carter* series, which also introduced the detective genre to motion pictures. From this six-part Éclair film's inception in 1908, through subsequent spin-offs like *Dr. Phantom* and *Zigomar*, audiences were enthralled by weekly installments of mystery and murder. The adventures of Nick Carter, "King of Detectives," made a fortune for Éclair over the next several years, becoming the most eagerly followed serial until the advent of Pathe's blockbuster cliff-hangers of the mid-1910s.

Other movies produced by Éclair became near epics in the hands of leading directors Georges Hatot, Victorin Jassin and especially Maurice Tourneur, whose cinematography may have been the most beautiful of the early silent period (not surprising from a pupil of sculptor August Rodin). With the enormous success of the *Nick Carter* pictures, Éclair's capital skyrocketed from 500,000 francs to over a million francs in the span of less than a year, permitting the company to enlarge its lavish 14-acre studio site at Epinay. Despite the mainstream appeal of its private eye yarns, Éclair maintained a highbrow reputation for elegant period movies like 1909's *The Legend of the Good Knight,* acclaimed for its imaginative use of light and shadow in scenes that underscored the impact of a lushly romantic 17th century plot. Éclair was also famous for the quality of the stories and subjects it chose to exploit. Long before Hollywood's campaign to acquire eminent authors as screenwriters, Éclair actively courted the contributions of such literary greats as Emile Zola, whose estate extended exclusive rights to the company to "cinematize" stories based on his novels.

In set design and all that went into creating mood or *mise en scene*, Éclair exerted a noticeable advantage over the competition. Formally trained artisans like Ben Carre and Wray Physioc produced inventively beautiful stages and props. Éclair was especially praised for its fashionable interior decorations, some of the most expensive to be seen in films at the time. Technically, Éclair pictures were highly advanced for the day. The studio's cinematographers, Rene Guissart, Georges Benot and Lucien Andriot, achieved stunning trick shots and other pioneering visuals with their state-of-the-art cameras and artistic methods of manipulating atmosphere through light and special angles. The Éclair photographers became known for their successful use of double exposure and dissolve methods, for introducing a forerunner of the traveling or panning shot, and for perfecting a close-up technique that involved two medium shots intercut by the close-up frame itself. Parallel editing, being experimented with by Griffith and other American filmmakers, had already been perfected by Éclair's cameramen. As another example of its commitment to the latest technology, Éclair was the first major producer to embrace science and nature subjects as popular cinema entertainment, releasing them on the same programs as dramatic stories and comedies.

The serials and other Éclair films were such a hit in America that a distribution branch was opened in New York in February 1910. Although the building of an elaborate production facility had been proposed early on, it was not until the spring of the following year that the company put these ambitious plans into action. On arriving in New York to inaugurate the construction of a fully functioning American studio at Fort Lee, Éclair's president, Charles Jourjon, announced his intention of "giving the trade an American picture made the Éclair way." His plan, he said, was to "marry the appeal of American acting to French technical mastery." Jourjon admitted that the personality and style of American actors would be as essential to Éclair's success as the filmmaking skill of his countrymen but he refused to comment on the types of players he was interested in engaging. Instead his interviews focused on the building of the Fort Lee plant, which he promised would be "the largest and most modern motion picture facility in the country."

Completed in late June, the Éclair studio may not have been the largest (Lubin possibly surpassed it in size) but its architecture and machinery were likely superior to anything in America at the time. In addition to a film-processing factory and laboratory, a storage vault and a workshop, all separately housed, there were two studios, both entirely glass-enclosed, with a profusion of stages and sets that would enable the shooting of as many as four films simultaneously. The 40,000-square foot main studio took up two whole blocks at Fort Lee. This building contained sets, dressing rooms and the company's business offices. It would eventually include the first animation laboratory in America, supervised by famed cartoonist Emile Cohl, and a special lab for producing color filmstock; using the British-patented Kinemacolour process Éclair produced the first natural color movie in America a year later.

In 1910-11 Eclair arrived on the American movie scene in a blaze of publicity that must have startled the growing but naïve industry. To modern eyes the company's press releases and advertisements, proclaiming Éclair "the world's greatest studios," seem bombastic. But Jourjon believed hype was key to getting the attention the new branch needed. Once properly noticed, he felt Éclair's superlative product would stand on its own. "Éclair inscribed on a film denotes a standard of excellence possible only through long experience and limitless capital," bragged an advertisement in the *Dramatic Mirror*. A full page notice in *Billboard* stated that Éclair "must and will make greater and better moving pictures until the world proclaims them absolutely the best. Then Éclair will strive to surpass itself."

The company would have been better advised to spend some of its 'limitless capital" on a good translator for its publicity department as some published advertisements betray a lack of understanding of the English language. For instance, posters and print ads, even Éclair's own office letterhead, used the clumsy tag "Branches Throughout the Earth" until early 1912. Even so, Éclair created a hubbub of interest, praise and inspiration in the movie trade as it prepared to compete with big American studios (and Fort Lee neighbors) like Biograph, Vitagraph, Selig and Kalem. After building drew to a close on the factory and studios at Fort Lee, a call for actors, advertised widely in the movie press, met with a euphoric reception from established and amateur players alike. Hundreds of actors – men, women and children – jammed the Éclair offices on West 27th Street.

Dorothy was not among the clamoring Manhattan throng responding to the big casting call that July. She had already been hired, having obtained a private interview with Éclair's general manager, Harry Raver, one of only two Americans involved in the company's upper administration. The meeting had been arranged through Dorothy's agent Pat Casey, who also represented top Broadway and vaudeville talents Al Jolson, Fanny Brice and Fred and Adele Astaire. Dorothy was signed for an estimated $125 a week, a sum comparable to that being earned by fellow rising star Mary Pickford, then appearing with Majestic Films. Despite her past work of only bit and supporting roles, Éclair's management was confident it could capitalize on Dorothy's fame as the "Harrison Fisher Girl." Many other gifted and attractive young women were hired, but Éclair chose Dorothy as the company's first American leading lady.

Press releases soon rang out the news of Eclair's fascinating new star. A writer for

MY QUEEN

Moving Picture News professed himself in awe over Dorothy's "faultless beauty:"

> *However, beauty of feature, coloring and form is not Miss Gibson's only charm. By conversing with her it is found that she is a most unassuming young woman ... Said Miss Gibson of her employers, "They are the most charming people to work for. I think the reason why I like my work so much now is because I have such nice people to work for."*

Other news articles were similarly enthusiastic. In one story, Dorothy was reported to have "forsaken the studio of the artist for that of the motion picture." *Moving Picture World* in its August 19, 1911 issue announced Dorothy's acquisition by Eclair, claiming Harrison Fisher "consented to Miss Gibson's acceptance of the flattering offer only on condition that she continue to pose for him twice a month."

Elsewhere it was said that Dorothy was "the prettiest of new photoplay talents," even that she was "poised to take her place among the most promising of picture personalities." As one columnist wrote:

> *The Éclair managers have expressed great faith in their inspired acquisition of the charming as well as beautiful young actress whose modesty is as apparent as her prettiness.*

Asked in the interview if she considered herself suited to the life of a "cinematic heroine," Dorothy replied that she was just an average girl and that "as to becoming a favorite in the moving pictures that remains to be seen." In several stories, Lubin and IMP were criticized for allowing Dorothy to languish in the background while Éclair was praised for "having secured her services." One journalist made a point to stress that, in spite of Dorothy's stage experience and celebrity as a model, she "was not permitted top roles" at the other studios. The *Moving Picture World* published a similar comment, adding that

> *the others failed to recognize her charming personality for its full worth and, consequently, missed a "one best bet" .... She is now destined to gain a much wider and more lasting reputation...."*

Of her signing with Éclair, Dorothy admitted that

> *I was having a fine time and was full of hope that I could make a success of the job. But it seemed more important to other people than to me, and I did not want to disappoint anybody.*

Meantime Éclair had gathered an impressive stock company, top players chosen for their recognition by audiences. Apart from nabbing Dorothy, Éclair hired two other well-known models – Helen Marten, who had won a "Gibson Girl" newspaper contest, and Lamar Johnstone, who had also posed for Charles Dana Gibson in a series of Arrow Collar advertisements. He joined Eclair as Edwin L. Johnstone but soon switched to the catchier "Lamar."

Rounding out the core group of actors who were to serve as Dorothy's costars were Alec B. Francis, a veteran British stage performer who went on to appear in many major films, even into the sound era; Julia Stuart, also English, who won a following for her hearty maternal roles; Guy Oliver, another seasoned character actor who would have a long career; and John G. "Jack" Adolfi, who distinguished himself later as a director. In addition, Éclair employed a number of ingenues for supporting and extra roles; among these were Isabel Lamon, Rolinda Bainbridge, Gussie Hunt, Margaret Severance, Virginia Rogers and Muriel Ostriche, who became a friend and confidante to Dorothy. By the end of July, the Éclair studios were in full swing at Fort Lee as preparations got underway for the company's first American release.

New Jersey's fabled Fort Lee film community, the precursor to big-time Hollywood, had been teeming with motion picture folk since about 1906. Before that, the borough of Fort Lee was known primarily as a resort destination, owing to its picturesque locale along the Hudson River. Banked by the Palisades Cliffs, Fort Lee offered nearby New Yorkers and savvy tourists a bucolic weekend or summertime retreat. As a small village of vacation cabins and inns sprang up, filmmakers were quick to recognize Fort Lee's idyllic and varied topographical features – cornfields, craggy shores, winding country roads, beautiful hills. Soon studios and laboratories were being built on Fort Lee's northern border, launching its brief but influential tenure as "America's first motion picture town."

As Professor Richard Koszarski of the Fort Lee Film Commission has lectured, Fort Lee had a great impact on the progress of American movies through the conflagration and collaboration of talent that first assembled in the tiny township. Moreover, Fort Lee was notable, he said, as the "dissemination point for French filmmakers," especially Éclair. "While filmmaking in Fort Lee did not strictly precede similar activity in Hollywood," said Koszarski, "this was the first industrial location in America completely dominated by the producing and printing of motion pictures." Éclair's facilities dominated this pioneering community of moviemakers, quartered as it was right in downtown Fort Lee. Dorothy was impressed by the huge Eclair plant but the responsibility she felt as the new company's leading lady was what occupied her thoughts. Privately she pined over not having found the man of her dreams, but as a leading actress she could play at lovemaking to her heart's content. It was so sudden, this new duty of being "the star." How would she adapt?

The challenge she and fellow cast members faced in communicating with their new French-speaking directors – and the rest of the crew with whom they worked closely – also became an abiding concern for Dorothy during her first days of assimilation at Fort Lee. As her costar Muriel Ostriche recalled, none of the directors or technicians could speak English so an interpreter, who was confused by American slang, was provided, though with sometimes hilarious results. Dorothy, too, recalled some funny and embarrassing moments when she and others of the cast tried to speak French:

I admit to making some very humiliating mistakes with my imperfect French, and

MY QUEEN

I remember what an effort it was on the part of those dear gentlemen not to laugh in my face.

Communication was crucial between the actors and directors Georges Le Soir and Etienne Arnaud, but the performers also had to converse with technical supervisors Henri Maurice and Georges Maire as well as chief cameramen Rene Guissart, Georges Benot and Lucien Andriot. As far as is known, the only interpreter Éclair sent to the Fort Lee branch was the long-suffering Louis Grisel, surviving photos of whom, taken on the set at Éclair, attest to his affability. The problem of intercommunication may well have contributed to manager Harry Raver's decision to engage a trio of freelance American directors – Lawrence McGill, James Slevin and William Haddock – to expedite production on the company's first release, an extravagant vehicle which president Jourjon had chosen to mark the debut of Éclair's U.S. branch. This film would prove more than Éclair's introduction to the American motion picture industry. It would confirm the appeal and marketability of the new-fangled feature film.

As a symbol of the unique cultural coalescing of brains and creativity that was taking place with the arrival of Éclair, an epic-scale historical drama, based on the American Revolution with sidelights on the important role France played in the colonies' liberation from Britain, was planned. Jourjon approved this story as ideal material for launching the studio after learning of the part New Jersey – and the Fort Lee area in particular – had played in the Revolution. General Washington had established headquarters at the garrison of Fort Lee during the 1776 campaign of the British Navy to seize New York and the Hudson Valley. It was at Fort Lee at the time of the Continental Army's fateful retreat from General Cornwallis' troops, that the famous words of pamphleteer Thomas Paine, then an aid to Washington, were written: "These are the times which try men's souls." The history of Fort Lee and his own desire to see a French-American bond glorified inspired Jourjon to back a film that would, as he put it, "show the love between our two nations." The two-reel film was to be called *Hands Across the Sea in '76,* later abridged to *Hands Across the Sea.*

Although former stage producer Lawrence McGill received sole credit for directing *Hands Across the Sea*, dramatist James Slevin directed portions of the film and wrote the script. According to Dorothy, William Haddock also helped direct this production, but his involvement hasn't been confirmed. *Hands Across the Sea* was a mammoth production, especially for such a new studio, and the movie press expressed amazement at the undertaking. But Éclair cast and crew – and a reputed 2,000 extras – had no time to be awed. A steady round of shooting began early in August at Fort Lee with later location shoots in Philadelphia and New York. According to studio publicity and reviews, the scenes in which Dorothy and her costars appeared were a series of expertly choreographed playlets, bathed in misty light, set against elaborate backdrops.

This cinematic form of *tableau vivant*, representing significant events in the War of Independence, was based on Slevin's script which was inspired by original historical accounts. A too-rigid reliance on facts and dates posed the threat of being cumbersome, but in the hands of McGill and cameramen like Andriot, a potentially boring costume play became what critics called a "spectral pageant," a "majestic parade of the ghosts of history and of the peace and power of liberty." Slevin's scenario called for a multitude of large-scale crowd scenes. These ranged from the convening of the first Continental Congress to Washington's taking command of his forces; and from Ambassador Franklin's reception at the Court of Louis XVI to the triumphal arrival in America of French military heroes Lafayette and Rochambeau, who declared their intention to fight with the colonists against England.

Other scenes treated emotional episodes like the British Navy's execution of Nathan Hale and the treason case of Benedict Arnold. Full-cast sequences of French court fetes and balls at Mount Vernon added a high-gloss elegance to Slevin's story, but the most memorable scenes were reserved for the recreation of the legendary battles of the Revolution – Monmouth, Brandywine and Yorktown.

Dorothy was assigned several focal roles in the various vignettes that made up *Hands Across the Sea* but the most consequential was that of Molly Pitcher, the beloved heroine of the June 1778 Battle of Monmouth. The wife of artilleryman William Hays, Mary "Molly" Hays had followed her husband into battle, soothing him and his fellow gunners during the hot summer conflict by bringing them pitchers of refreshing spring water, thus winning her famous nickname.

Molly Pitcher's efforts in quenching parched throats during the skirmish might have been sufficient to earn her a mention in history but she was destined to make a bigger mark. When she found her husband wounded at his cannon, she resolutely took the rammer from his hands and manned the gun herself. The feat allegedly won Molly a commendation from Washington. New Jersey-born Dorothy was eager to portray one of her state's proudest historical figures, and no actress could have asked for a more sensational entrance into a scene. Through swirling clouds of cannon fire, her skirt billowing about her, Dorothy's Molly emerges onto the bloody range of battle with her trusty pitcher. Hoping to succor soldiers from thirst, she confronts instead a moment of crisis as her husband collapses. Instinctively, she replaces him at his gun. Illustrator Percy Moran, who was commissioned by Éclair to paint a set of promotional cards and posters, interpreted in brilliant color Dorothy's characterization of Molly Pitcher. This painting illustrated a lavish brochure that formed part of Éclair's promotional package to exhibitors. "It was a very melodramatic part, and the newspapers talked a great deal (about it)," Dorothy recalled of her historical impersonation. "I spoke to a women's club once about Mollie (sic) Pitcher, and they listened to me as though I was a reincarnation. All because of a few feet of film!"

Dorothy was also featured prominently in a scene set at the Palace of Versailles, in which Benjamin Franklin (played by William Corbett) was presented to Louis and Marie Antoinette. Based on a story told in the memoirs of the Queen's lady-in-waiting, Madame Campan, the Slevin script called for Their Majesties to command the most beautiful woman present at the ceremony to bestow a wreath of laurel on the head of the American statesman. A rococo Dorothy — powdered, bewigged and attired in the pannier fashion of the day – is chosen by fellow courtiers from the crowd. Authentic even to the painted mole on her cheek, she steps gaily forward and, with a dainty curtsy and shy smile, fulfills the royal summons.

MY QUEEN

Two other tableaux in *Hands Across the Sea* that starred Dorothy were referred to in later reviews as poignant moments in the story. In the first, Dorothy and another actress play maidens threatened with rape by intoxicated soldiers who have surrounded their cottage. General Washington (Darwin Karr) comes to their rescue, fighting off the attack of the men from the steps of the house. The *New York Dramatic Mirror* critic wrote that this shocking instance of sexual violence was handled sensitively. A surviving still of this scene conveys its tension and something of the strength of Dorothy's screen presence. Dorothy looms at the top of the home's front porch stairs, clinging to a pillar, while Karr stands below her, brandishing a knife to protect her against the marauders. A maid and another woman (possibly Helen Marten) cower behind her. They have retreated in terror but she stands boldly before her attackers. In the second touching scene, Dorothy plays the widow of a soldier at whose flag-draped grave she kneels, praying and weeping, their two children at her side. Lost in her grief, her head is bowed and her hands clasped. As her son and daughter look into her stricken face, a consoling officer wraps his cloak around them.

Hands Across the Sea met with overwhelming popular and critical acclaim, making it one of the most successful films of 1911. Long before its release, which was delayed due to editing changes from November 7 to November 21, the press reflected the picture trade's anticipation. Throughout filming, the columns of the *Dramatic Mirror* constantly referred to the movie's progress, commenting that "great interest is manifested in it," even that it was "awaited with unusual interest," while *Billboard* frankly admitted that Éclair's debut "is creating quite a stir in film circles." *Billboard* also predicted that, owing to the amount of time and expense going into the production, a "spectacular and thrilling film is assured." Although two reels in length and thus qualifying as a feature in those days, *Hands Across the Sea* was released as a regular issue to theatres and film exchanges, saving them the added cost generally charged for "specials" or "extras." This was an original marketing move, and it paid off. Exhibitors across the country reported phenomenal bookings and box office receipts on opening night.

The *Moving Picture World* published a notice that as far away as the Lyric Theatre in Fort Wayne, Indiana, *Hands Across the Sea* had been "greeted by rounds of applause," moreover that "hundreds of people (were) turned away." The Midwest's biggest film broker, the Standard Film Exchange of Chicago, ordered two copies of the picture to meet an overwhelming demand for bookings and, according to Eclair, also bought "the largest quantity of posters ever placed for a regular release in the history of films." Even accounting for the hyperbole of Éclair's publicity office, *Hands Across the Sea*'s positive reception from exhibitors and patrons was enormous. The media showered it with praise. *Moving Picture News*' November 18 issue, beating the competition to print by a week, devoted its cover to *Hands Across the Sea*, choosing a still of the French court scene of Dorothy anointing costar William Corbett with laurel leaves.

Reviews were ecstatic. *Moving Picture News* opined that Éclair had "scored a great success" with *Hands Across the Sea*, which represented "a proud step forward" for the industry:

> *Much more marvelous than a masterpiece from the painter's brush is this living picture of bygone days. Just as an historical drama is presented to us in the theatre,*

is this wonderful film given to us by Éclair, only with more vivid reality even, because we have the actual battle scene given us, showing all its terrible consequence to man and beast. The scene, "Before Yorktown," and the battlefield after the battle, with women moving quietly among the dead and dying, ministering to the comfort of the surviving ones, stand out by themselves as masterpieces of motion picture photography and intelligent artistic production.

Billboard wrote that the "production itself is a monstrous one, deserving much more than the 2,000 feet of film allotted to it, having been put on at a very greatly augmented cost and with hundreds of cannon, horses and war equipment." *Billboard*'s critic, who attended an advance screening in New York, said in the magazine's November 25 issue that "the most remarkable features of the film are the photography and splendid outdoor scenes." Despite what the reviewer called "an overabundance of military scenes," he pronounced *Hands Across the Sea* "exceptionally accurate, splendid in design and finely finished," pointing out its "completeness" and "air of reality."

The *Dramatic Mirror* concluded that the film "possesses many elements of excellence which give promise of a really high standard of production by this company." While acknowledging the technical accomplishments of the director and cinematographers, the publication declared that the "historical characters are represented by players of distinction." *Moving Picture News* concurred, singling out Dorothy for her role as Molly Pitcher. Of the scenes in *Hands Across the Sea* that were mentioned as particularly strong, one was considered extremely inventive by critics. A dream sequence, apparently a prologue to the story (though this isn't clear from reviews), was expertly handled in its depiction of Washington contemplating the future. The "unique innovation" of trick photography permitted a "visionary" episode "in which the skyline of New York is seen to rise out of the open sea."

For all its merits, Éclair's first American feature was not without flaws or controversial elements. Some writers challenged the historical basis for the portrayal of Washington as having a "romantic disposition" and the taste of the inclusion of fictional heroine Charlotte Temple's sexual indiscretion was questioned. Moreover, the error of using inauthentic national flags throughout the first reel, and in a battle scene in the second half of the film, was criticized. That aside, Éclair secured a solid financial and creative hit. Jourjon's hopes of success for his French-American experiment had been realized. As *Billboard* stated, the film signalized a new bond in filmmaking as "America stretches out her hand in love and gratitude to France, the friendly nation across the sea."

Chapter 4:
Bows Attract Beaus
1911-1912

HAVING WOWED HARD-NOSE exhibitors and the fickle public, Éclair's *Hands Across the Sea* established the studio's viability in America. The company took out full-page notices in *Moving Picture News* and *Billboard,* thanking the trade and fans for ensuring a "signal and unprecedented success." A spate of advertisements followed, informing the industry of the new Eclair release schedule – Tuesdays were reserved for dramas, Thursdays for comedies, and Sundays for a variety of films imported from the Paris studio. Éclair had arrived.

While *Hands Across the Sea* was a feature-length offering, all of Éclair's subsequent vehicles were one-reelers, the average length for films at the time. As with Biograph and Vitagraph, Éclair's most conspicuous rivals in the U.S. market, the French-based firm is considered by cinema historians to have brought the one-reel picture to "a zenith of excellence in execution." It's ironic then that a company best known for its "shorts" would have raised the bar on the appeal and marketability of features. Though not the first feature film to be shown in America, *Hands Across the Sea* was the most publicized and popular, giving Uncle Sam's stamp of approval on the emerging genre.

The production values of Éclair movies – especially their tonal and atmospheric quality – also set a steep technological standard in America after the opening of *Hands Across the Sea.* As has been shown, a high stock was applied to advertising, too. Éclair's promotional strategy may have been ostentatious, but it was effectual. What surprised the trade most was that the same amount of care and expense that Éclair lavished on its debut film was now going into booming its regular roster of comedies and dramas. *Billboard,* in its November 4, 1911 issue, made special note of the impression this level of advertising was having on the industry:

> *The manner in which the films are being announced is the cause of attention for they are being exploited almost the same as some of the big feature films of three or more reels in length.*

For every film released it was reported that Éclair was supplying exhibitors and exchange offices with huge lobby posters and banners, illustrated brochures or "heralds," and sets of stills and lobby cards. The posters were lithographed in six colors, an expensive process bypassed by most filmmakers, and the cards were color-tinted or else finished in glossy sepia hues. Supplemented by eye-catching print ads in the daily press and weekly entertainment magazines, Éclair's marketing campaign was probably the most effective of any undertaken by an American studio at that time.

Dorothy was reaping the rewards of the publicity Éclair was accruing. Advertisements offered special display portraits of Dorothy to exhibitors and exchanges as incentives for ordering Éclair films. These "handsome art photos of the Harrison Fisher Girl" were sent free of charge to "all theatres and brokers who inquire after Éclair brochures." The press published these pictures in rapid succession just before and in the wake of the premier of *Hands Across the Sea*. In fact Dorothy Gibson items appeared steadily in the press throughout the end of 1911 and well into the following year. One photo of her was featured so often that Dorothy asked her agent to stop issuing it.

> *There was a photograph which the newspapers used constantly, and I hated it. I told Pat Casey to withdraw it. If I was sick of it, I was sure everyone was. So others were substituted.*

The picture to which she referred was a beautiful oval portrait of herself in classical pose, wearing chiffon draperies that swathed her shoulders and a wreath of flowers in her hair. This picture is still the most familiar image of Dorothy, reproduced in a number of books and articles. Dorothy might have been tired of seeing that photo, but it was to its widespread dissemination that she owed the mixed blessing of a fateful introduction to the man who would change her life.

She couldn't have dreamt up a more romantic meeting, although the liaison that resulted was no fairytale. Her first sight of the dapper older man who would rule her heart was a moment more glamorous than any movie scene in which she had performed. Dorothy didn't detect the pitfall that awaited her; she was too enthralled to care. In an instant, she fell completely and catastrophically in love. "It happened before I knew it," she told writer Adela Rogers St. Johns in 1934. "Only in youth can we love so much and so unwisely." Millionaire Jules Brulatour stepped into Dorothy Gibson's unsuspecting world barely a month before her starring debut in *Hands Across the Sea*. The occasion was the second annual ball of the Motion Picture Distributing and Sales Company, of which Brulatour was president. It was Saturday night, October 14, 1911, and New York's elegant Alhambra Hall, decorated in colorful silk banners and strips of variegated tissue, overflowed with the movie glitterati of the day – men in cutaway coats or the new tuxedos, and women in trailing pastel creations. As *Billboard* reported:

> *The reception hall was well crowded by an enthusiastic audience, which demanded encore after encore of music and song .... Enthusiasm for the first dance would not subside and, amongst a swirl of dream-producing music, assembled friends formed the line for the grand march. Everything became terpsichorean and the light fantastic kept up its noble work well into daybreak of the next morning....*

BOWS ATTRACT BEAUS

Jules Brulatour, as head of the Sales Company, presided as the party's host. A well-tailored dinner jacket revealing his athletic physique, the 41-year-old film mogul made the rounds of his guests until at some point on that festive eve he met young Dorothy.

Escorted by Éclair's Harry Raver, Dorothy was having the time of her life — dancing, singing, chatting and laughing. Presumably it was Raver who introduced the star to their host. Enchanted by Dorothy's blue eyes and slender figure, Brulatour told her that he felt he already knew her, having "admired your lovely photo in the papers." Suddenly the party didn't matter so much, and the pair fell into conversation. "After I met Mr. Brulatour, I do not think we stopped talking," Dorothy said later. "It was that kind of immediate acquaintance where no one else exists." Dorothy was captivated by Brulatour's courtly Southern drawl and penetrating dark eyes, and despite his dignity, there was a boyish charm in his manner. Was this not the man of her dreams? For the Machiavellian Brulatour, Dorothy was a vision, a temptress — and after he beheld her on the screen, she became even more of a prize.

It's extraordinary the two had not met before. In addition to directing the Sales Company, the leading motion picture distribution firm in America, Brulatour was an advisor and unofficial producer for Éclair. Perhaps he hadn't visited the studios at Fort Lee during the filming of *Hands Across the Sea*, which was already wrapping up by the time of the Sales Company ball. Or if he had, he was content to admire Dorothy from afar. But now they had met and, as night stretched into the following day and into the first weeks of a whirlwind courtship, Brulatour made it clear he was wildly interested in the young actress. According to Muriel Ostriche, Brulatour was more than infatuated with Dorothy – he was "in love" with her. As an equally smitten Dorothy reveled in the passion of those first days of their romance, she had a lot to learn about the man who was to become the greatest, and most annihilative, influence on her life.

Born Pierre Ernest Jules Brulatour in New Orleans in 1870, the lover who conquered Dorothy's heart rose from clever entrepreneur to brilliant businessman. Wealthy at a young age through savvy investments and slick salesmanship, he was ambitious, stubborn, suave, handsome — and married.

With his wife, Clara Isabelle, whom he wed in 1894, Jules fathered two daughters, Marie Ruth and Yvonne as well as a son, Claude Jules. In 1898 the Brulatour family moved to New York, where Jules found himself managing shipments of foreign motion picture projection equipment and supplies. His entrance into the burgeoning film trade, which some sources claim occurred before he left New Orleans, was a critical decision that would someday land him at the top of the business. Late in 1907 Brulatour's career began its upward swing when the Paris-based Lumiere Freres offered him a job as its chief American representative for the sale of motion picture stock to the increasing number of filmmakers operating in New York. Jules, who was not only of French descent but conversant in the language, was a shoe-in as Lumiere's U.S. agent. He traveled to Paris to meet with his employers, learn about their product, and to sign an exclusive contract with Lumiere, returning in March 1908 to open Lumiere's manufacturing plant in Vermont. Jules also launched an advertising campaign that brought him to the fore of a brewing controversy in the hierarchy of the movie trade.

In 1908 battle lines were being drawn between a powerful association of film producers, the Motion Picture Patents Company, and a growing, but as yet unorganized, group of independent filmmakers. Brulatour was soon at the center of the storm and making a fortune out of it. The Motion Picture Patents Company, led by redoubtable inventors George Eastman, founder of Eastman Kodak, and Thomas Edison, had resolved themselves into a cartel comprised of a notoriously hand-picked selection of studios that claimed exclusive rights to the use of certain moving image projection machinery and film stock.

The Patents Company ruled exhibitors and exchanges with an iron legal fist, insisting on high operational license fees and stiff penalties for showing independent films. Law suits were both threatened and carried out by the so-called "Edison Trust" against many independent movie companies, most notably the IMP studios run by Dorothy's old boss, Carl Laemmle. A Bavarian immigrant who started his own nickelodeon and distribution outlet in Chicago, Laemmle moved his business to New York only to be forced out of business through intimidation from the Patents Company. In Laemmle, the trust had an impassioned crusader who railed against the monopoly held by Edison, Eastman and their colleagues – the "Sacred Eight" of American movie makers. These included the heads of Biograph, Vitagraph, Kalem, Selig and Lubin studios. The threats, scare tactics and other methods of intimidation indulged in by the Patents Company were legion. As Q. David Bowers has written in his biography of Dorothy's Éclair costar, Muriel Ostriche:

> The independents had to be ingenious and often their filming was conducted in secret at unannounced locations to escape spies for the trust who were ever on the lookout for misuse of cameras employing trust-owned patents.

Brulatour walked bravely into the fray when he offered his services as sole agent for Lumiere film stock to the disenfranchised independents, thus bypassing the restrictions imposed on them by the Patents Company, which refused to sell Eastman stock to any but their elite membership. For a year, Brulatour ran his agency almost single-handedly out of a small office on Broadway, selling Lumiere film to companies excluded by the Edison-Eastman bloc. He became renowned for his "cash up front" deals, off the top of which he skimmed a hefty profit. "Many myths have grown up about how much Brulatour netted for each foot of film he sold," wrote *Variety* some years later, "ranging from a half cent to one penny per. Actually he received many times less than either figure, his big profits stemming from immense volume and quick turnover plus his intimate knowledge of the then-pioneering industry."

While cashing in, Brulatour cemented friendships that would prove advantageous. One of these new associates, Laemmle, now in charge of his own studio, saw in Brulatour the partner he needed to fight the trust. Hoping to enlist the newcomer as a champion of his cause to defeat the old guard, Laemmle called on Brulatour with a proposal to consolidate the independent producers under the aegis of an alternative distribution agency to the Patents Company. The independents, he said, had been waiting for an opportunity to unite in opposition to the Edison-Eastman faction, and they felt Brulatour had the power to formalize the revolt. Brulatour agreed to join forces with Laemmle, and on March 20, 1909 the men formed the Motion Picture Distributing and Sales Company. With Brulatour as president, the Sales Company offered independent filmmakers, exhibitors and brokers the option they wanted – to operate without unfair tariffs and limitations and to be assured of legal protection when threatened by the trust. The movie companies in particular were ecstatic that they wouldn't have to rely on low quality film stock anymore but could acquire high grade imported Lumiere film through Brulatour. The action Brulatour and Laemmle took by establishing the Sales Company signaled a death knell for the Edison Trust.

The first to realize this was its main backer, George Eastman, who saw his patented safety film losing prestige with the encroachment of Lumiere. Eastman decided to strike a deal. As the Patents Company's hold on exhibitors and filmmakers dwindled, Eastman felt he had to make a move or risk losing the market entirely to the French. He contacted Brulatour and offered him an exclusive contract to sell Eastman film to the independent filmmakers, cutting in finally on Lumiere's threatened stronghold.

Brulatour accepted. Never above a little deception where there was money to be made, he couldn't resist playing both sides of a gainful situation. Continuing to market Lumiere supplies, while also selling Eastman products ("right through the back door," as one critic put it), this scheme was accomplished easily enough through his convenient purchasing formula of cash only. Soon Brulatour exchanged his Lumiere agency for Eastman entirely and eventually became a close friend (and frequent financial supporter) of the "Kodak King." Their personal friendship had been affirmed by spring 1910 when, through his recent involvement with Éclair studios, Brulatour prevailed upon Eastman to relocate his continental storage facility to the Éclair plant near Paris. This badge of honor for Éclair led to Jules' unfettered influence with the company, which he served as advisor, spokesman and producer over the next five years.

This, in a gilded nutshell, was the story of her lover's rise to prominence that Dorothy learned during the formative weeks of their liaison. In a short time, Jules Brulatour had become one of the most powerful figures in the American movie industry. The *Dramatic Mirror,* in a profile of Brulatour the following year, wrote that he was "the type of businessman who lends dignity and credit" to an enterprise, adding that he was "earnest and conscientious in the discharge of his duties as the head of the chief independent organization." *Billboard* further commented that "the motion picture business is practically controlled by the two great rival companies, the Motion Picture Patents Company and the Motion Picture Distributing and Sales Company."

The praise was accurate but so is the fact that Jules, while a pioneering force in early cinema, was a ruthless, even corrupt, executive. Despite his magnetism socially, he wasn't so charming in the boardroom. Not only did he dishonor his contracts with Lumiere Freres and Eastman Kodak in 1909 but during the First World War, when he was appointed to President Woodrow Wilson's Committee of Public Information, he was investigated for bribing fellow members; nothing was proven, but he resigned under pressure. As late as 1924, after assuming the presidency of Kodak, the Federal Trade Commission fined Brulatour and George Eastman for "conspiracy to hinder and restrain commercial competition." It isn't surprising, perhaps, that Jules' business dealings were less than honest when his private life involved dividing time between his family and a mistress.

Clara Brulatour wouldn't find out about her husband's dalliance with Dorothy Gibson until late 1911 or early 1912. The affair devastated her and their children – 16-year-old Ruth, 6-year-old Yvonne and 4-year-old Claude. While Jules' son and daughters went on to lead apparently happy lives, Clara never recovered from the degradation of his infidelity, played out as it would be in the nation's headlines. As for Dorothy, as much as one can admire her as an actress, it's hard to sympathize with the private role she played as paramour. She was young and naïve, that's true, and her later words indicate her regret. But at the time, Dorothy does not appear to have considered anything but her overwhelming feelings of adoration for Jules. Dreams of marrying Brulatour blocked out the reality of her predicament. Complicating the situation, the status of her own marriage to George Battier is unclear; although separated, they weren't divorced yet. If Dorothy failed to take into account the consequences for Jules' family, she also doesn't seem to have realized the danger in which she placed herself by trusting in a man capable of such deceit. In this way, her long romance with Jules Brulatour is as central to understanding the private Dorothy as is her relationship with her mother, the other guiding (and not always benevolent) force in her world. Jules, the prime player on Dorothy's most vulnerable stage, would chart her life's erratic course. Like Pauline, Jules loved Dorothy. He spoiled her, he cultivated her, and he ruined her.

As her romance with Jules matured and her career progressed during the fall of 1911, serious thoughts were far from Dorothy's mind. Having Jules' love filled her with happiness, giving her energy and focus in her work, especially after he declared his intention to leave Clara and the kids and marry her. Dorothy's friend Muriel expressed amazement that Jules planned to abandon his family for her. But Dorothy believed him. The exhilaration Dorothy derived from her new love resulted in a stream of top-notch performances in popular movies that confirmed critics' glowing predictions for Éclair's success and her own. *Hands Across the Sea* had introduced Dorothy as a leading lady but not as a star, since the movie's epic pageantry and cinematography outshone the efforts of individual actors. The first movie to showcase Dorothy's beauty, personality, and acting ability was *Miss Masquerader*, released on November 28 and advertised as a "rollicking natural comedy." Filmed concurrently with *Hands Across the Sea* and originally planned for release November 11, *Miss Masquerader* was only the second American vehicle for Éclair, which placed faith in the story's viability as a starring vehicle for Dorothy. That faith was justified. It's a shame this film is lost; reviews indicate it was highly amusing.

Miss Masquerader, a society farce in which a young heiress, played by Dorothy, tires of the insincere attentions of money-hungry suitors and schemes to find the perfect beau, provided audiences with many laughs. In a surprising cross-dressing angle for the day, the heroine, who is "out for a lark," disguises herself as a man and with the connivance of her uncle goes to a country club to pick out a potential winner on the sly. She meets the object of her desire, and becomes his chum. The storyline avoids any homosexual subtext by providing a secondary plot in which the girl, attired as herself, is given an opportunity to meet the man she's chosen. But after he suspects she is seeing another man, he becomes depressed and writes for advice to his pal from the club. The film concludes as the mischievous heiress shows up at her boyfriend's house to reveal her prank.

Dorothy won rave reviews from critics for this exercise in romantic burlesque. As *Billboard* wrote, Dorothy revealed herself as a "lovable, vigorous specimen of budding girlhood" and turned in a bravura performance of "laughable situations," like cavorting about golf links and a tavern "bundled up in male attire." The reviewer also liked her in the love scenes in which she "figures triumphantly." *Moving Picture News* called *Miss Masquerader* a "delightfully humorous picture" in which "exquisite photographic value is apparent in every scene." It recommended the movie as the ideal "remedy for overworked mortals who tire of the grind and long for an excuse for laughter to brighten their weary souls." The *Moving Picture World*'s December 9 issue found the movie "fun," mentioning that it contained "some very pretty lovemaking," was "splendidly acted as a light society comedy" and had "considerable charm." A longer separate review in the *World* praised the film's "good comedy situations," which permitted "both photographer and players an opportunity to produce a succession of clever effects." Dorothy's screen presence and refreshingly placid acting style was singled out:

> It is in comedy — high-class comedy — that Miss Dorothy is destined to shine; that she can shine with all her charming, winsome manner, is sufficiently proved by her appearance in the Éclair comedy, Miss Masquerader....The story is very slight yet it affords Miss Gibson an excellent opportunity to show us what she can do.... Especially noticeable is the reposeful work of Miss Dorothy. She has acquired the knack of expressing herself without excessive gesture or facial contortion, a failing so common among photoplayers and so distressing to those who view them. Miss Gibson is to be congratulated on her singular ability .... If the pace of Miss Masquerader is kept up, Éclair comedies and Miss Gibson will be prime favorites with photoplay enthusiasts."

Moving Picture News also praised Dorothy's realistic acting:

> Miss Gibson's work in this comedy is very fine, and special mention should be made of the perfectly natural manner which is a feature of her acting. Splendid poise was displayed by Miss Gibson throughout.

Rounding out the more extensive reviews for *Miss Masquerader*, the *Dramatic Mirror* stated that the "setting, the backgrounds and the manner in which this pleasing little comedy is put on make it an altogether delightful and entertaining one."

One criticism stands out, however, and is open for speculation now. The *Dramatic Mirror*'s writer said that the final scene in which the heiress reveals her escapade to her beau "was not as capably or effectively managed as might be." In light of the fact that Dorothy's comparatively undemonstrative acting was new to audiences, perhaps it was the subtlety of emotion and gesture she used in this scene that confounded the critic. Not all reviewers were surprised by Dorothy's special technique which, while rare, was shared by at least one other rising star. Echoing the opinion of the reporter for the *Moving Picture World*, entertainment journalist Hazel Simpson Naylor, in a syndicated January 1912 article in the

FINDING DOROTHY

Hearst press, announced that:

> As with Miss Mary Pickford, no frenzied gesticulations mar the photodrama portrayals of the Éclair American stock players' new leading lady, Miss Dorothy Gibson.

Dorothy was cheered by the hearty reception awarded *Miss Masquerader* and shared her happiness with "Julie," the nickname with which she teased her lover. Their secret moments aren't recorded, except that they made frequent nocturnal visits to "discreet" hotels like the St. Regis and the Great Northern. "I met her in a clandestine way in order that our relations might be concealed." Jules later admitted of his affair with Dorothy. "During this period, she beguiled me to be more and more in her company, and acquired an increasing domination and control over me and finally mastered my will and dictated my actions."

Julie accompanied Dorothy to the studio parties she regularly arranged with Muriel and other costars, and at the Motion Picture Exhibitors Ball that year, where Dorothy "sang several old English songs," Brulatour was present (but so was Clara). Fashionable New York restaurants like Sherry's and Delmonico's were known to offer special rooms to gentlemen who chose to dine with women other than their wives, so this was probably another outlet for Julie and Dorothy. Like an entranced schoolboy, Brulatour found a way to see her often and adopted a pet name of his own for Dorothy – she became his "Mutsie."

Chirping love words by night, the pair worked hard by day. Brulatour attended to his duties as top rep for Eastman Kodak, as head of the Sales Company and as a producer for Éclair. In addition to assisting in the defense of the Chicago Film Exchange against Thomas Edison and his monolithic trust of producers, Brulatour was also challenging New York Mayor William Gaynor's proposed ordinance to severely restrict operating licenses for movie theatres. Meanwhile, Dorothy was busy "emoting" in her own original way before the cranking cameras of the Éclair studio at Fort Lee. There was "very little of the glamour connected with movie stars," Dorothy recalled, when she and other cast members were working on a film. Pushing oneself into states of glee or sadness many times a day, depending on the number of "takes" required to get a scene just as the director wished, was strenuous. She also recalled the searing heat of the glass-roofed stages combined with the electric lighting of the sets. An added complication was the problem of communication with the French directors and cameramen. The latter shouted instructions to the interpreter, who would then attempt to translate them to the actors. The result was an "aggravating routine of stop and go," as Dorothy put it. At least she and her costars and the crew with whom they worked all got along well. In between takes, Dorothy and Muriel munched on chocolate caramels and practiced the new ragtime steps; Muriel was so proficient at dancing that everyone on the set called her the "Turkey Trot Girl." The actresses also carried on a good-natured competition to see who would be pictured next in the film magazines.

An example of the camaraderie that prevailed on the set at Éclair is found in the way a certain shy typist employed in the administration office was coddled by her coworkers. This woman, Violet Johnson, wanted to be a "picture star but was so timid she could not raise her voice," as Dorothy recalled. Still, Violet responded to every casting call. She was rejected each time but instead of making fun of her, Dorothy, Muriel and others consoled her and made sure to invite her to their parties. On the bulletin board beside the woman's desk were always notes of affection from the stars and directors, including a funny one from William Haddock, which read: "My dear Miss Johnson, when the occasion presents itself for the necessity of photographing a whisper, I shall certainly call you." The sense of community at Éclair – studio picnics, games, sleigh rides and costume parties – brought Dorothy close to Harry Raver, who had been a carnival representative before taking over the management of Éclair. Following his tenure with Éclair, he financed a number of other independent movies and managed several more studios. He had a penchant for backing news-related or celebrity-oriented films, such as a documentary on the Vatican and a movie based on Upton Sinclair's *The Jungle*, in which Raver persuaded the author to make a cameo appearance.

Dorothy also grew close to Etienne Arnaud, who would alternate with Lawrence McGill, Jay Hunt and William Haddock as director of the films in which she starred. Arnaud, well known for making historical and biblical stories, was lured by Éclair from competitor Gaumont. There he had directed the controversial *Bluebeard*, which was withdrawn and re-edited for its violence, and a well-received color-tinted biography of Napoleon. Arnaud was dispatched from the Paris studio of Éclair to the American plant in late 1911. Reports stated that he was "shipped post-haste" to Fort Lee where he was "placed in full charge" of the Éclair studio. The tone of the press stories hinted that there may have been turmoil at the American Éclair, which Arnaud was expected to quell. His own first films would not be released until February but Arnaud did implement several blanket changes that took effect immediately. He vetoed the consideration of Western-themed scenarios and concentrated on scripts with social or political commentary such as were contained in the domestic dramas and comedies that had made Éclair so famous in France. He also followed the lead of Éclair's home office in buying the film rights to famous novels and plays.

On December 12, while Arnaud contemplated his first American project, Dorothy's third film was released, and the seventh to be launched by Éclair. That week *Billboard* paid tribute to the "leading moving picture actors" with a photomontage in which Dorothy's portrait was featured first and topmost, dominating images of fellow stars Florence Lawrence, Maurice Costello, Max Linder, Alice Joyce and Mary Pickford. At the same time, Brulatour did his bit to aid Dorothy's career by arranging for her photo (the one he adored and she hated) to form the cover of a "movie star picture book," the publication of which he was financing as part of a special publicity package for his clients. If Dorothy thought these honors were a sign that another batch of rave reviews lay ahead for her new movie, she was mistaken.

The Musician's Daughter, directed by Jay Hunt, was a flop. Inexplicably billed as "An American Drama," it received negative reviews (when it was reviewed at all), and Éclair took notice. Luckily for Dorothy, she wasn't the star of this film, which called for a juvenile female lead. Grace Scott filled the role, apparently very inadequately at that, and she was dropped from the stock company after this production. Dorothy had only a cameo in *The Musician's Daughter*, in which she plays a fairy godmother of a prima donna who teaches the heroine voice elocution. This movie's rather complicated story line involves an aging composer (William S. Rising) who goes mad and is institutionalized after his wife dies, only to be restored to sanity when their daughter becomes a famous opera star. The *Dramatic Mirror* said the basic plot was "convincing and effective" but thought the acting was "throughout affected and labored, especially that of the leading lady," moreover that the story was "not well told." The *Moving Picture World* was the lone voice of praise, finding the film "very touching" and claiming Dorothy played her role of a "dissatisfied prima donna" to "a nicety."

The failure of *The Musician's Daughter* underlined Arnaud's insistence on better material for scripts and determined the Éclair management to see that he got it. In January 1912, Éclair augmented its already extravagant publicity budget by a reputed $10,000. Films to be boomed were *The Wrong Bottle, Mamie Bolton, Love Finds a Way* and Victorien Sardou's *Divorcons,* all starring Dorothy and directed by Jay Hunt. Each of the four films was well received by critics and the public, putting Éclair back on track. Advertisements for another Eclair film released at this time, *The Doctor's Duty*, cited Dorothy as its star but reviews don't mention her and she does not appear in surviving scene stills.

Released January 2, *Divorcons* was the first film version of the famous French three-act comedy about a wife's dalliance that receives the support of her husband. The twist is that the husband has a method to his apparent madness. In the Éclair script Dorothy's flirtation with a "juvenile fop of a cousin" is condoned because the husband theorizes that without the threat of exposure the thrill of romance will fizzle. His ploy works. Dorothy's character loses interest in the admirer and returns to her husband. But the lover is not to be thrown over and he pursues the couple to a fashionable café where he confronts the husband. A fight ensues, the cad is flung out of the restaurant, and the married pair embraces in a "lasting reconciliation." The *Moving Picture World* called the movie "exquisite" and "ingenious." A surviving scene still reveals something of Dorothy's coquettish charm. Smiling sweetly, she brazenly extends her hand to be kissed by her beau while her husband and a friend look on in amazement.

Dorothy's next film was a domestic melodrama, and she welcomed the chance to show she was proficient in the genre. So far movie fans had only seen her in an historical part, comedic sketches and a brief dramatic cameo. *The Wrong Bottle* offered Dorothy her first emotional role in a modern setting. In *The Wrong Bottle*, Dorothy plays an impoverished widow who falls sick in a sweat shop. Her young daughter, looking after her at home, goes to the pharmacy with a prescription but is given the wrong vial of medicine. The druggist, realizing his mistake in handing the girl a bottle of poison, rushes after her, reaching the bedside of the ailing woman just in time to save her and to realize she is a former childhood sweetheart. Reviews were unanimous that the film was "well-acted and carefully constructed," and "artistic and commendable," one critic noting that the picture cast a "very pleasing impression" on audiences. Dorothy was back as a comedienne in *Mamie Bolton,* released January 16. She portrays a suspicious wife who imagines her husband is having an affair when she reads a telegram addressed to him that refers to a "Mamie Bolton." It turns out the name is that of a goldmine in which her husband has invested stock, not another woman. But in her excitement the young wife doesn't read the note thoroughly, and telephones her father and mother to rescue her from her disgrace. The frantic parents arrive to avenge their daughter's honor while the husband, just returned home from his office, tries to explain the misunderstanding. Finally realizing the telegram she has misread actually assures her husband he has made a fortune out of the Mamie Bolton Mine, Dorothy convinces her father to cease his oratory on the shame of adultery, and her mother to drop the gun she has grabbed to force her cheating son-in-law out of the house. Billed as "A Veritable Fun Fest," the movie was evidently a hit. "Wall Street is still laughing," one critic wrote. Another review considered the "comedy atmosphere well maintained," adding that it "never falls to coarseness."

As a comedy, Dorothy's next picture, *Love Finds a Way*, was as romantic as it was rollicking, repeating the formula that had made a success of *Miss Masquerader.* Dorothy plays Helen, an impecunious former debutante who must now seek work to support herself and her mother. Helen finds employment as a maid to the wealthy Mrs. Gray, whose handsome son, Fred (acted by Lamar Johnstone), falls "desperately in love" with her. The pair's romance is discovered by Fred's irate mother who orders Helen out of the house. Thinking she's rid herself of the unworthy imp, Mrs. Gray places an advertisement for another housekeeper, specifying that applicants be "middle aged." But Fred schemes to get his girlfriend rehired and disguises her as a much older woman. The hysterical end to the story comes when Mrs. Gray takes Helen back unawares, only to have her husband fall for the maid this time.

Most reviews for *Love Finds a Way* left out the whimsical conclusion which, as *Moving Picture News* wrote, "is too good to tell here." *Billboard* likewise teased readers. "There is a surprise for those who see this film," hinted the magazine's January 20 issue. The *Dramatic Mirror* called the movie a "sprightly and entertaining little comedy," finding the closing scene, when "the father stepped in to make love to (Helen)," an uproarious touch. Dorothy was again complimented on her acting, which the *Dramatic Mirror* said was carried out "with a pleasing grace and naturalness." While *Billboard* commented on her "beauty and refinement," the *Morning Telegraph* made a point to commend her unique screen style:

> *Miss Gibson controls herself admirably in tense moments, making but measured use of her hands. In scenes wherein she must register elation, there is none of the wild twirling about and grotesque expressions of other photoplayers, but a simple gathering smile and a characteristic lifting of the eyes, which casts its spell.*

Love Finds a Way was also notable for serving as Lamar Johnstone's debut as a leading player and the beginning of his popular screen partnership with Dorothy Gibson. During the run of *Love Finds a Way*, Dorothy made an unplanned – but historic – public appearance at Weber's Theatre, where she went one evening to see the newsreels. Joined by her mother and two girlfriends, Dorothy was spotted in the audience by the theatre's manager, Bernard White, who asked her if he "might present her to his house." Dorothy consented and White introduced her on stage before the show. As she was handed a bouquet of roses, the "crowd of picturegoers" clapped out an "affectionate welcome."

Wearing a pale blue evening frock and a headdress of pearls, Dorothy gave a short, impromptu speech – one of the first instances of a film star addressing fans in a public venue. Only Florence Lawrence is known to have made a similar appearance during these early days of the star system. "I am pleased to be with you tonight," Dorothy said, all smiles and allure. "I am in as much anticipation of the program as you are, and I am certain we shall have a wonderful time together. My congratulations to Mr. White and his employees, who always put on the best pictures in town, even when they are not my own!" As Dorothy laughed with her host, she was wildly applauded. Newspapers reported the following day that:

> *Miss Gibson then returned to her balcony box and was observed throughout the exhibition kindly acknowledging the curious glances of members of the public who could not refrain from watching their heroine as she watched the pictures right along with them.*

Back at Fort Lee, Dorothy was eager to start work on her next film. *The Awakening*, released February 6, was her chance to portray another emotional role. Directed by William Haddock from a "social message" script approved by Etienne Arnaud, the majority of the film took the form of a dream sequence. Leading man Lamar Johnstone plays a just-graduated college student who's on his way home to a party planned by his parents (Guy Oliver and Florence Hale), sister (Rolinda Bainbridge) and fiancee (Dorothy). But a friend (Darwin Karr) persuades him to stop in at a pub before returning and he gets drunk, in which condition he returns to his parents' home, collapsing in a stupor over the table of refreshments his loved ones have prepared. He dreams he's still at the bar where he witnesses his sweetheart accepting the advances of his pal. Pulling out a gun, he attempts to shoot the man but the bullet strikes his girlfriend and kills her. He's tried and convicted for her murder and sentenced to be hanged. At this point, the young man awakens from his dream and, on being embraced by his family and the girl he loves, he vows to mend his dissolute ways.

Even more of a tear-jerker than *The Wrong Bottle,* the movie established Lamar Johnstone and Dorothy Gibson as powerful leads. *The Awakening*'s frank treatment of the vice of alcoholism and its social consequence was hailed as a triumph and the entire cast was awarded accolades for their moving performances. A publicity photo taken on the set of the film, showing the full cast and crew, including director Haddock, cameramen Benot and Andriot, even interpreter Grisel, conveys the emotion of the tale in the expressions and body language of the subjects. Johnstone received most of the attention for his inspired portrayal of the central character but critics considered Dorothy effective in her role, especially in the scene of the hero's intoxicated arrival home, in which she receives him "lovingly, sadly." She must have relished the fullness of her part in *The Awakening,* being allowed to play both an adoring maiden and a creature who was, as the *Dramatic Mirror* described her, "by no means the sweet, pure-minded girl." The *Moving Picture World* found the piece "very well acted" and commended the cinematography, notably the opening shot filmed on location at the College of the City of New York. Aware that exhibitors might be concerned about the adult subject matter in *The Awakening*, the *World* assured readers that the movie was "a safe feature and can be advertised as such." The *Dramatic Mirror*'s opinion summed up most reviews:

> *Reformations of dreams are not, as a rule, extremely convincing picture dramas,*

43

BOWS ATTRACT BEAUS

but this little play has been performed with a certain human depth that at once arouses the sympathies.

After completing this film, Dorothy took a short break from the studio, concentrating on her own unfolding off-screen drama. Brulatour was having a successful run himself. On February 10, Julie's Sales Company released the first episode of the *Animated Weekly* newsreel, which he personally produced. It was a project he had been working on for many months, and he was proud to see it come to fruition.

A week later Julie won a landmark suit against the Patents Company, a case that had been in the courts for two years. His Sales Company had gone to trial in defense of its client, Laemmle, who was contesting the claim of the Edison Trust that IMP studios had unlawfully used equipment protected by patents owned by the combine. The New York Supreme Court dismissed Edison's bill of complaint, stating that neither Brulatour nor Laemmle had infringed on Patents Company copyrights.

It was also about this time that Harry Raver struck up a deal with Julie to split the interests of the Sales Company. By this arrangement, which would not end amicably, Raver assumed directorship of a subsidiary interest called the Motion Picture Sales and Supply Company, which would handle new accounts and market a special line of Eastman Kodak products. For the time being, their partnership seemed a solid one. On top of everything else, Brulatour entered into an alliance with Éclair president Charles Jourjon to start a new production firm, Peerless Features (later Peerless Pictures). Operated as an extension of Éclair for a short period, it eventually moved into its own building.

Meanwhile Brulatour and Dorothy continued their secreted suppers and hotel visits, and exchanged love letters and telegrams using their Julie and Mutsie aliases. They took long drives together in Brulatour's big touring sedan along the country roads of Fort Lee or Long Island, where he had a summer place. In time he presented Dorothy with a special gift — her very own vehicle, a little electric town car, painted gray with an interior of pastel chintz. Dorothy was ecstatic. The dainty confection of an auto was perfect for her shopping trips, lunch dates with friends, and for meeting Julie wherever and whenever he desired. Lost in her excitement, Dorothy couldn't have known what an unhappy memory that beautiful car would one day be.

Following a week's rest, Dorothy was back at Éclair. Her return was critical: Etienne Arnaud was ready to direct his first two films, *The Guardian Angel* and *Bridge*, and Dorothy was his choice for the female lead in both vehicles. Some critics had expressed worry that Arnaud's style would fail to appeal to American audiences but their fear was unfounded. Both films proved unqualified hits. *The Guardian Angel* especially resonated with the public. The story of a poor but talented violinist (Johnstone) and his wife (Dorothy), each of whom become attracted to wealthy benefactors, was a sophisticated drama with an emotional dimension. The couple's little daughter is the titular angel as it is thoughts of her that save her parents from infidelity. "They both meet at the cradle of the sleeping child," the *Moving Picture World* wrote, "and complete love is restored." The magazine complimented the "form and atmosphere" of the picture, adding that the story was a "beautiful subject, delicately portrayed, and entitled to a leading position on any program." *Bridge* was another domestic melodrama that pleased the public and received good notices from critics. Encouraged by a girlfriend, a young wife (Dorothy) spends her afternoons playing the "sinful society game of bridge," and losing a lot of money at it. Afraid to tell her husband about her losses, she borrows cash to settle her debts from a scoundrel who's interested in her, using the collateral of a pearl necklace. Thinking he has her cornered, the cad tries to blackmail her, threatening to expose her financial misdeeds unless she agrees to elope with him. In the end the wife decides to come clean about her bad bridge playing and is forgiven by her husband. Reviews considered *Bridge* "competently acted" throughout its "many original and startling situations," and praised the film's "striking effects in lighting, photography and coloring." In keeping with Arnaud's prestige and Dorothy's popularity, a number of stills from *Bridge* and *The Guardian Angel* were published in trade journals and the mainstream press. Dorothy didn't recall the names of her first Arnaud films but she said the distinguished director was a "true professional" and "guided me so well I am sure those pictures were among my best work."

In contrast to her high-brow efforts for Arnaud, Dorothy's next project was a fast-paced, Jay Hunt-directed comedy. *Getting Dad Married,* the story of a young woman, Ellen, played by Dorothy, scheming to find a new wife for her widowed father, was a hilarious success, and extant stills hint at the movie's high level of action. Another comedy, *The Kodak Contest,* proved a hit, too. In a convoluted attempt at slapstick, the story involves a newspaper photo contest in which the antics of a newlywed couple, played by Dorothy and Darwin Karr, are unwitting catalysts. *The Kodak Contest* was one of several Éclair films which Julie produced that year, and its title certainly suggests he took special interest in it. In *The Kodak Contest,* as the young husband is helping a heavy-set black woman carry bundles of laundry across a street, his picture is snapped by freelance photographer Kodak Kittie (Helen Marten) and published in the morning edition of a local paper. Across town, his bride, who's out shopping, is frightened by menacing hobo Weary Jones (Jack Adolfi) sauntering in an alley. As she faints in a policeman's arms, her picture is taken by another contestant. The photo makes it into the evening's edition. The wife sees her husband's picture and, feeling humiliated, prepares to leave him. The husband sees his wife's picture while at work and returns home to have it out with her. Finding her packing her bags, he quarrels with her but softens when he sees a set of baby clothes among the things she's packing. The plot seems clownish today and the reference to the black woman is racist, but *The Kodak Contest* was a winner with exhibitors on its release March 14.

"The complications in this well-produced comedy are both unique and amusing," opined the *Dramatic Mirror.* "It is well set and played." *Moving Picture News* agreed:

> The Kodak Contest *is a story replete with laughable situations sure to prove popular as a good finishing reel for the best of programs.*

Dorothy had a chance to further hone her dramatic skills in her next assignments, two penetrating stories scheduled for back-to-back release – *It Pays to Be Kind,* directed by Arnaud, and *A Living Memory,* which costar Alec Francis directed. The first of these was one of the social commentaries dear to Arnaud's heart. Reviews and surviving stills indicate that it was a remarkable piece of aesthetic filmmaking. It was notable for another reason – Dorothy was not its star. In a gesture that shows her malleable spirit, she appeared in a supporting role to ingenue Isabel Lamon, the daughter of another Éclair actress, Mathilde Baring. No doubt due to the neglect she had suffered at Lubin and IMP studios, Dorothy was happy to allow the young actress an opportunity to reveal her gifts in a story tailored to her.

It Pays to Be Kind, written by G.T. Evans and billed as "A Sermon Drama to Young Girls," was widely promoted in the trade papers. It was the tale of a wealthy Philadelphia widow, Mrs. Burt (Julia Stuart) who, in mourning the loss of her daughter, wishes to take on as a companion one of her four estranged and pampered nieces, played by Dorothy, Rolinda Bainbridge, Gussie Hunt and Lamon, the youngest of the girls. To test their graciousness and charity of heart, the aunt visits the New York home of her brother Charles (Guy Oliver) and introduces herself to his daughters as a poor relation. The elder sisters airily decide she must replace the cook whom they have discharged but the youngest niece is kind and thoughtful. Learning all she needs to know, Mrs. Burt returns home and asks her brother (who seems to have been in on the plan) and his daughters to tea. When the party arrives, the girls are astonished to find their aunt living in a mansion. They're further mortified when Mrs. Burt selects the youngest of them as the one who will take her daughter's place in her home.

Reviews for *It Pays To Be Kind*, released March 19, congratulated the efforts of Isabel Lamon and Julia Stuart in the lead roles but the characters of the selfish sisters were also praised. The *Dramatic Mirror* thought their acting was "commendable for making (their) attitude thoughtlessly human instead of theatrically cruel." The *Dramatic Mirror* went on to say that the "production is put on with much care, is given interesting treatment, and furthermore is acted with much freshness and spirit." Dorothy especially appears to have excelled at bringing depth to the character of the sister she portrayed in *It Pays To Be Kind*. In surviving stills, her expressions reveal a heightened sensitivity to the action that's taking place around her. She seems sympathetic in the scene where the old aunt is being put to work in the kitchen and to be deeply hurt in the closing scene when her younger sister is picked to live in luxury. The film's moral was clear. *Moving Picture News* concluded in its preview synopsis: "The (sisters) return to New York sadder but wiser girls."

After *It Pays to Be Kind*, Dorothy resumed her duties as Éclair's leading lady in the romantic drama *A Living Memory,* the heart-warming tale of a bachelor, John Ransome (Alec Francis) who cherishes bygone days spent with his boyhood sweetheart. To his shock, Ransome learns of her death and that she's sending him her daughter (Dorothy) for him to look after. When the young woman arrives, he finds she is her mother's "exact image." Although he soon falls in love with the girl, who seems to share his feelings, Ransome is self-conscious of his age and tries to interest her in one of his younger friends. But the ruse fails and she declares her love for the older man. *A Living Memory,* released March 26, won more great reviews for Dorothy's serene acting style. Enthused the *Dramatic Mirror* critic:

> *A human little sketch from life is most capably suggested in this film, bringing forth the underlying thought with a taste and delicacy in which the setting and mechanical effects, together with the expressive acting, have no small part. Mr. Francis and Miss Gibson present these leading roles with fine intelligence and discrimination.*

A Living Memory, promoted as an "art film" by Éclair, received large orders from exhibitors

FINDING DOROTHY

nationwide but similar pictures weren't forthcoming, and Dorothy was given another slapstick comedy to put over. In *The White Aprons,* Dorothy plays Miss Beth, a cooking school teacher, who is smitten with the administrator and tries to impress him with her mincemeat pies. She succeeds but his widening belly necessitates a diet. Rather than offend his sweetheart by asking her not to bake any more pies, he buries them in the garden where Miss Beth's pupils discover them near their vegetable patch. The teacher is outraged but in learning her suitor's reason for rejecting her cooking, the pair make up. The *Moving Picture World* considered it only a "very slight" story that "will pass as filler."

Notwithstanding lukewarm reviews for *The White Aprons,* Dorothy was in top form as an actress by April 1912 (and making a then whopping $275 a week) but the hectic shooting routine she was keeping up exhausted her. She was also becoming more dependent on Julie to fulfill her off-screen happiness, confiding to Muriel that she was thinking of retiring from acting to spend more time with him. The change of heart reflected in her loss of interest in work seems sudden, perhaps due to some developing issue with Julie. Before asking Raver to relieve her from some of her assignments so she could take a vacation, Dorothy finished making another burlesque-style comedy, *Brooms and Dustpans.* Unfortunately, this movie turned out as badly as Dorothy was feeling and, to judge by the reviews it got, it was probably the worst she ever made (not surprising given such an uninspired title). Advertised as a "Merry Story with a Point," *Brooms and Dustpans* actually made little sense. A banker (Gladden Jones) is angry with his son (Guy Oliver) for not taking an interest in the family business. The son retaliates by selling broomsticks door to door, hoping to embarrass his father. The whole family is soon so infuriated with the young man that they prevail upon a "kissing cousin" (Dorothy) to "get his goat" by selling dustpans door to door. The two meet on the street armed with their household wares and have a fight. But the man proposes an answer to the dilemma by sweeping an engagement ring into his sweetheart's dustpan. This otherwise unmemorable film was interesting for cameo appearances made by Éclair director Lawrence McGill and interpreter Louis Grisel. Others in the cast were Mathilde Baring and Julia Stuart. "One cannot confess to being highly entertained by this intended comedy," the *Dramatic Mirror* reported on April 3. "It is rather flat and absurd from the viewpoint of story and presentation…. It is very much wanting in dramatic form. Half the film is subtitles."

What action was lacking on screen was rife in Dorothy's personal life by the time she finished filming *Brooms and Dustpans.* Having by now appealed to Raver to release her for a short period, she confessed to him she was thinking of quitting the studio. Raver told her she just needed some time to herself, and her agent Pat Casey advised against "taking a hasty step." Raver frankly explained to Dorothy that he had no one to stand in as leading lady, and asked her to at least give him time to find a replacement. Jules also encouraged her to stay on at Éclair and as an incentive offered to foot the bill for a six week vacation in Italy. "I was feeling very run down and everyone insisted I go away for a while," Dorothy said many years later. "So Mr. Brulatour made arrangements for me to have a wondrous holiday abroad. It seemed the ideal solution." Raver agreed to let her go, but asked her to complete three "quick comedies," as Dorothy remembered. She admitted she "raced through the pictures" and "did not give my best."

These movies, *The Lucky Holdup, The Easter Bonnet* and *The Revenge of the Silk*

47

Masks were all released either during or just after Dorothy's return from Italy. But there was a fourth picture included in the mix, a drama based on a beloved classic that somehow eluded Dorothy's memory. *The Legend of Sleepy Hollow* was only the second filming of Washington Irving's creepy tale but the production met with a disappointing reception, which may be why Dorothy didn't remember it. The *Moving Picture World* reviewed it as a "fair feature" that was "well photographed," but admitted it "isn't exciting," moreover that "the Headless Horseman won't fool even the children." The *Dramatic Mirror* panned it as a choppy and disjointed offering, materially worsened by an "overuse of subtitles." Dorothy's role in *The Legend of Sleepy Hollow* is unclear but advertisements for the film, booming her as the "Harrison Fisher Girl," indicate she had a leading part.

The Lucky Holdup, the first of the trio of comedies Dorothy was assigned, was a frolicsome story, and ninety years later it became the first of the star's lost films to be discovered, rescued by collectors David and Margo Navone, and preserved by the American Film Institute in cooperation with the Library of Congress Motion Picture Conservation Center. So far *The Lucky Holdup* is the only Dorothy Gibson movie known to exist, although even it isn't completely intact, some four minutes of running time having been cut by the unknown exhibitor that once owned it. Dorothy could never have guessed that an audience a century into the future would be served their first sampling of her celluloid self in this quaint action-adventure-comedy. Not much is known about the making of the movie, and Dorothy didn't remember anything special about it either. But to silent screen buffs there is a lot that's special about the eight minutes that remain of *The Lucky Holdup*'s original twelve minutes of raucous fun and suspense. The best thing is Dorothy as she smiles her adorable way through this rare one-reel treasure. *The Lucky Holdup*, as the title on the surviving print reads, was actually registered and advertised as *A Lucky Hold-Up,* released April 11, just as Dorothy was heading home from her European jaunt. Billed as "The Comical Tale of Cupid's Victory Over a Highwayman," the story was a frenzied one.

In the movie, Miss Barton (Dorothy) and her beau Mr. Chapin (played as usual by dapper Johnstone) find themselves caught up in a feud between their affluent families. Their fathers are partners in a brokerage firm and come to blows over a deal. While at a banquet some time later, on seeing their children dancing, the embittered old men demand the young lovers end their courtship at once. The couple, refusing to do so, elopes out West to a place "in the mountains" called Bear Gulch where they're robbed by two bandits and taken to their hideaway. The kidnapped youths convince the robbers to send a letter with a demand for money to their respective parents, who unite in a common goal to rescue their children. The old men, on arriving at Bear Gulch, are held up by the same thieves but on awarding them a $5,000 ransom, they're reunited with their children. The closing title card reads, "All's well that ends well."

The Lucky Holdup wasn't as widely reviewed or advertised as other Éclair films starring Dorothy, and what critical analysis it won wasn't entirely positive. The *Dramatic Mirror* critic wrote that

FINDING DOROTHY

Assuredly there is both humor and novelty in this little farce conception, and the play has been constructed to bring out the amusing complications which arise.

While *Billboard* found the conclusion effective, the *Dramatic Mirror* thought it was "not strictly American in conception." The *Dramatic Mirror* reviewer also found the photography less than impressive and that there was a "want of spirit displayed in the actors." Since the whole film is not extant, it's impossible to give a thorough critique today. Nearly half of the scenes are missing, including the dance sequence at the beginning and the part of the story that takes place in the thieves' mountain cabin.

Of at least fourteen title cards describing the action, only nine are in place. More disappointingly, the surviving footage is severely deteriorated throughout. Despite the missing frames excised by an exhibitor to fit it into a tight program, and other drawbacks, the film is surprisingly effective as a comedy. Filmed entirely at Fort Lee, both in town and in the surrounding woods, the movie is remarkable for the example it gives of Éclair's reputation for ideal lighting and clear photography. It is also beautifully tinted in shades of blue, green, yellow and rose. That this is still apparent in such a ravaged print is a testament to the excellence of the restoration work done by the Triage Film Lab. Most importantly, *The Lucky Holdup* allows fans of silent movies to acquaint themselves with the moving image of Dorothy Gibson and to judge her on-screen abilities. She doesn't have much time to exhibit a full range of emotion in this picture, but she proves to viewers that she had a refreshingly natural method of performing. Dorothy's mannerisms and gestures are subtle and her facial expressions, especially her rather naughty smile, are beguiling. In this movie, whatever one may think of the unfolding story, it's a treat to witness the star's personal magnetism at work. It's also interesting to note her fashionable wardrobe, namely a taffeta dress with an open neck and three-quarter sleeves, a fur-trimmed velvet coat and a plumed hat. In a costuming flub common in the early silent era, Dorothy had already worn the coat and hat in at least two films; stills record them in *Divorcons* and *It Pays to be Kind.*

Probably Dorothy's finest moment in *The Lucky Holdup* is a scene set at a bank where she and her new husband discover they've run out of money for their little escapade. Seated before the teller's desk, Johnstone's character confesses that his account is dry. Aggravated, his bride insists they must have more cash. Johnstone pulls a dollar out of his pocket, and hands it to Dorothy. His lips can be read as he says, "One!" Dorothy wears a look of disgust and her words, too, are easy to discern: "Is that all?" she asks, and leans her head sulkily on her hand. Contemporary criticism of the acting in this vehicle as lacking in spirit seems unjustified. All four principals — Dorothy, Johnstone, Guy Oliver as Dorothy's doting father and Alec Francis as Johnstone's ill-tempered dad — each go through their scenes with admirable restraint. Johnstone is particularly winning as a strapping collegiate type, and Dorothy is more than convincing as his pampered wife. But it may have been the cast's very naturalness that seemed lackluster to some critics, accustomed as they were to other players' more "stagy" style. Additional Éclair stock members glimpsed in *The Lucky Holdup* are Jack Adolfi as a clerk, Isabel Lamon as a maid, and Julia Stuart in an unidentified role in the few seconds that remain of the party scene.

On the heels of *The Lucky Holdup* came *The Easter Bonnet,* to be released April

25. Despite the rush that was put on this production, considerable publicity was expended on it and a number of mostly positive reviews were published. The film paired Dorothy with Lamar Johnstone as lovers again, and it was the first time that her friend Muriel received second billing in one of her films. *The Easter Bonnet* tells the story of a "pretty little milliner" named Dora (Dorothy) who longs to own a new hat for Easter. When "haughty heiress" Agnes (Muriel) buys the hat that the milliner wants for herself, Dora copies it before sending the original to the customer. However, in the commotion of remaking and packaging, Dora orders the hat delivered to the wrong client by mistake. The result is that Agnes, after seeing Dora wearing what she imagines is her hat, sues the bonnet maker for theft. Enter handsome attorney Jack Barlow (Johnstone), Agnes' fiance. During the ensuing case, Jack falls for Dora whom he champions and clears of all suspicion. As *Billboard* encapsulated the plot in its synopsis: "It is the story of a rich girl who loses her sweetheart by her disdainfulness and conceit."

A still from *The Easter Bonnet,* published in *Moving Picture News,* reveals an enraptured Dorothy trying on her new hat while saleswoman Julia Stuart looks cautiously on. Muriel, according to one review, appeared in two roles in this film using split-image photography, but it's unclear what the second role was. In the last film she shot before sailing for Europe, Dorothy had little to do, appearing only in a few brief scenes. Yet it would turn out to be a more important role than she realized.

The Revenge of the Silk Masks, from a gangster script Arnaud wrote, was the second installment of a three-part "mini-serial" about the misadventures of a band of criminals called the Silk Masks and their rivals, a trio of hilariously named do-gooders, Kid, Kit and Kittie. This was another one of Muriel Ostriche's early starring vehicles. She plays Kittie, the girlfriend of Kid (John Troyano), a cowboy hat-wearing hero who is the nemeses of the Silk Masks' leader, Ralph. The couple's sidekick, Kit (George Larkin), does some undercover work to free Kittie from jail after Ralph has framed her for stealing a diamond necklace from a wealthy young matron (Dorothy). Kid, Kit and Kittie escape the clutches of the Silk Masks in this installment, but their foes are in hot pursuit, thus allowing for the next, and concluding, episode. The climax of the second installment takes place in court, and a still of this scene that appeared in the *Moving Picture World,* shows Dorothy looking appropriately haughty as the judge (Alec Francis) delivers his verdict. The photo also shows Dorothy once again sporting the trusty fur coat and hat she had worn in *The Lucky Holdup.* Until the introduction of studio-maintained costume departments in the 1920s, actresses arranged their own wardrobes with the annoying result that some pieces were repeatedly screened.

Like *The Easter Bonnet, The Revenge of the Silk Masks* featured "some excellent trick photographs." According to the *Moving Picture World*, the film was "fun" and "seemed to be liked" by audiences. Though forgotten today, the *Silk Masks* films were ahead of their time. The serial genre had been launched in France by Éclair, but was not yet being exploited by American filmmakers. The "Kid, Kit and Kittie" adventures didn't amount to a full-fledged serial in the mold of the *Nick Carter* films, but they were a small step in that direction. Arnaud's experiment became not just the first serial the Fort Lee branch of Éclair would undertake, but was the first to be produced by any American studio. Along with *What Happened to Mary,* the extensive 12-part Edison serial released later that year, Éclair's unassuming little "gangster chapter play" was a foretaste of a lucrative genre in American motion pictures.

Dorothy wasn't interested in making history when she wrapped up shooting on this film. But that's exactly what she was destined to do, though in a way she could never have imagined. "I was thrilled to finish up the pictures, and I started for Europe immediately," she said. "I took my mother and we looked (forward) to a glorious time." Dorothy bid farewell to her friends and coworkers at Éclair, to her stepfather and to Julie, who was unable to join her and expressed regret that she was leaving him for even a short while. However, he was wise to the news angle of the event and planned to have his *Animated Weekly* cameramen ready at the dock when she came back. He couldn't have realized how big the story of her homecoming would turn out to be. Dorothy and Pauline departed New York Harbor on March 17, full of expectations. What memorable experiences lay ahead in the Old World for mother and daughter on their first overseas trip? Whatever they were, none could equal the adventure their return voyage held in store.

Éclair press releases assured readers that "the popular leading photoplayer" was leaving for only a period of "rest and recuperation" and would soon return to the screen and her fans. Some reports claimed her itinerary was to include Egypt and the Algiers. It may have but Dorothy and Pauline only got as far as Italy when, on April 8, they received from Julie an urgent cable at their hotel in Genoa. The women had just come from Venice when they received Julie's wire. His message stated that Dorothy was expected back at the studio within two weeks to start filming a round of movies which Arnaud and his assistant, Maurice Tourneur, needed to expedite. It was a fateful summons. The greatest role of her career awaited.

Chapter 5:

Hands Across the Sea
1912

FROM GENOA, DOROTHY and Pauline arrived in Paris, concluding their month's touring of Italy's splendors. For Dorothy, solidly in the grip of love, the prospect of ending her European vacation was free of the regret she might have felt had she not been consoled by thoughts of returning to Julie. After booking first class accommodation for their voyage home, it was with glad expectation that Dorothy and Pauline flung themselves into shopping along the rue de la Paix, searching out last-minute additions to their new spring wardrobes. Regarding her purchases as a veritable trousseau with which to dazzle her waiting lover, Dorothy flitted between the smart fashion salons, brimming with the season's latest frocks. Dorothy had learned much as a model for Harrison Fisher and her taste was impeccable. Among the expensive designer clothes she bought were a champagne-colored afternoon dress, a pink chiffon and lace blouse, a velvet suit, a taffeta "pannier" dress, and a sleek white silk evening gown that would prove memorable for more than its fashionable label. The most conspicuous items in the trunks Dorothy hurriedly packed for the trip back to New York were six exquisite blouses of fine Irish crochet lace, complete with interchangeable lace collars and cuffs. Yet these weren't nearly as special as the silk stockings and frothy lingerie sets she had bought in anticipation of her reunion with Julie.

The Gibsons were scheduled to sail from Cherbourg on April 10. The ship they were to board may not have conveyed much to mother and daughter before they set eyes on it in the early evening hours. Whether or not they had read much about the White Star leviathan and its maiden voyage, the ladies were sure to be awed by their first sight of the magnificent vessel dropping anchor in the harbor. Emerging from the Paris boat train at Cherbourg, Dorothy and Pauline gazed across the bay. But there was no ship awaiting them as they had expected. They learned that a minor but ominous accident while departing Southampton Harbor at noon that day had delayed their ship's crossing the Channel. The force of the wake of its engines had popped the mooring ropes of a nearby boat, which then had drifted dangerously close to the new liner before being rebuffed by rescuing tugs. After an hour, as the shadows of evening gathered in the seaport, Dorothy and Pauline watched as the great ship, escorted by a gaggle of seagulls, finally hove into sight. With whistles bellowing and the sea churning about its massive hull, throwing up a cascading mist of sea spray, the ship made the most of its fashionably late entrance. Nothing could have been more impressive. There, silhouetted against the dusk sky, decks twinkling with lights, was the fabulous *Titanic*.

However impressive the great ship sparkling on the water seemed, it was still only a ship to the bored, impatient actress. For Dorothy, the *Titanic* represented seven days of whiling away her time before being reunited with Julie. Seeing him again was all she could think about. As the tender *Nomadic* left the pier and steamed out into the bay, laden with the glitterati of three continents, their servants, dogs and luggage, Dorothy's mind and heart were already in New York. As she would later tell a reporter for *Moving Picture News,* she felt "like a new woman."

"The ship was glorious," Dorothy recalled in a still later account. "Yet I was so homesick that my thoughts were not on my surroundings but on getting home. As the little boat took us out to the big ship, I was so happy at the prospect I couldn't think." It's fitting that Dorothy's introduction to the *Titanic* that evening should have been experienced in a romantic haze. On the blissful night that the star of the screen beheld the star of the seas, the *Titanic* was itself a dream of romance. Like Dorothy, the *Titanic* was brand-new to the world and faced a career full of promise. While an oblivious Dorothy longed for a rendezvous with her lover, fate ensured only an intimate embrace of horror for the radiantly unsuspecting *Titanic*. What a contrast to their ethereal first meeting when five nights later from a comparable distance, a lifeboated Dorothy witnessed the *Titanic*'s agonizing final hours. No longer lost in reverie, Dorothy would observe with emotion the destruction of the spectacular new ship, the lives of 1,500 people, and the confidence of an era.

Boarding the *Titanic* at Cherbourg that night, Dorothy and her mother marveled at the beauty of the liner. "It was the most wonderful steamship ever launched," she would enthuse to the *Morning Telegraph*. "Womanlike, I could not help but admire the furnishings." More is known of Dorothy and Pauline's experiences on the *Titanic* during the first days of the crossing than is true of many other passengers. Yet there are gaps in the record. Did the Gibsons first make friends while exploring the ship, as passengers do at the start of a sailing? Was fellow traveler Helen Churchill Candee, the interior designer and art critic, referring to high-spirited Dorothy when she later referred in a magazine story to "the most beautiful girl" among the passengers? Were Dorothy and her mother in the crowd on deck buying lace from dealers who came aboard during the ship's stop at Queenstown the following afternoon? Dorothy's love of crochet may well have tempted her to supplement her collection. If she indulged, it's safe to assume she didn't spend $800 on a single piece of Irish lace as is alleged of another *Titanic* celebrity — Madeleine Astor, wife of multimillionaire Colonel John Jacob Astor IV. Dorothy was doing well for herself, to be sure, but that kind of expenditure was still beyond her means.

In the bevy of fellow famous faces on the *Titanic* — tycoons, politicians, writers, artists, athletes, aristocrats — Dorothy found several who had also achieved prominence in the entertainment world. Foremost among these was Broadway impresario Henry B. Harris, travelling with his wife Renee. There were also opera manager Emil Brandeis, Albert A.

Stewart, a lithographer much in demand in the theatrical field, and two European singers, Ninette Aubart and Berthe de Villiers, both mistresses to wealthy men en route. There were even three other passengers with ties to the motion picture industry aboard. Daniel Marvin, son of Henry N. Marvin, president of the maverick U.S. movie studio Biograph, best known for shaping the genius of director D.W. Griffith, was returning home with his wife from their honeymoon. Independent filmmaker William Harbeck, noted throughout Europe for his travelogues and nature documentaries, had joined the ship at Southampton. Harbeck had been hired by White Star to film the maiden voyage; the line planned to have a tug take him off the ship in New York Harbor so that he could film the *Titanic* as it docked. And Noel Malachard, a cinematographer associated with Pathe Freres, was also on the *Titanic* especially to record the maiden voyage for his company's newsreel series. None of these men would survive the disaster.

Time aboard seems to have passed happily enough for Dorothy and Pauline. The pair socialized in the lounge, playing bridge, and enjoyed festive meals in the dining saloon where their table companions, including the *Titanic*'s builder Thomas Andrews, were no doubt charmed by the actress' cheerful personality. Dorothy, looking lovely in a black evening dress one night and a pink and gold gown the next, her hair dressed in matching bandeaux, must have enjoyed hearing Andrews' first-hand views about the design and performance of his marvelous ship. Likewise, he and the others — a Canadian honeymoon couple, Albert and Vera Dick — would have been fascinated to learn of Dorothy's work in the burgeoning industry of motion pictures. One wonders, however, if Dorothy's eccentric mother expressed at table her political views as boisterously as she would in after years.

By day, mother and daughter played bridge with various acquaintances, including Frederic K. Seward, a New York corporate attorney whom they knew, having attended church together. Seward, 34, a Columbia University graduate, was also a successful investor and well-known civic leader in Queens. Dorothy liked him, and they enjoyed laughing and talking together over tea, lunch, or their favored game of cards. She later claimed she "beat him at bridge every time and he loved it."

In the evenings, the Gibsons always took a brisk stroll about the promenade deck before retiring to their stateroom, No. 22, on the starboard side of E Deck. On April 12, the *Titanic*'s first full day at sea, Dorothy was overjoyed to receive a wireless telegram from Julie. His sparsely worded message of adoration read: "Will do everything make you completely happy, love you madly, Julie." Conversation during that night's walk on deck included Dorothy's hopes that Julie would soon acquire a divorce so they could marry, and the prospect of her retirement from acting to begin a new life with him. "It was a happy time," she would muse, made happier by yet another ardent cable from her lover the next day: "It cause no happiness without Mutsie, never allow you leave again, Julie."

By April 14, Dorothy and Pauline had settled into their own shipboard routine. It was Sunday, and as both had been active in church back home, it's possible they attended the interdenominational service held that morning in the lounge, presided over by the *Ti-*

FINDING DOROTHY

tanic's jolly-looking, bearded commander, Captain E. J. Smith. At some point in the day, Dorothy visited the Marconi office on the boat deck to send a message to Julie, acknowledging his wires. It read: "Hardly wait get back, cable made me awfully happy, Mutsie." It was transmitted at 6:45 p.m. Incidentally, Dorothy had received a third message, sent earlier that day, from Julie who informed her that he had reserved for their reunion adjoining rooms at the Great Northern Hotel.

Activities for Dorothy and her mother that day may have included shuffleboard, tea in the Palm Court, relaxing with a book in the reading and writing room, lunch in the *a la carte* restaurant, and more walks around the promenade. At one stage in the voyage, Dorothy performed impromptu in the lounge, singing to the violin accompaniment of another young woman, possibly 23-year-old Marjorie Newell, who was travelling with her father and older sister. Dorothy remembered that the other passengers who assembled to hear them "seemed to welcome our little concert."

Wherever they went and whomever they met, the topic of conversation was the ship's sudden increase in speed. The rumor circulating was that the *Titanic* was going to reach New York a day ahead of schedule and possibly recapture for her owners the coveted Blue Riband. Much debate would ensue about the truth of this plan but Dorothy, when interviewed by the press later, was adamant on the point. "It is useless to deny that the *Titanic* was out to break the transatlantic record," she told journalist Chauncey Parsons. "Everybody knew it. It was the talk of the voyage. Although four different boats had warned us of icebergs, we were going faster than ever." She claimed the *Titanic* was racing so fast that her speed "would be good time for a train." It should be noted that leading *Titanic* historians doubt that the White Star Line was actually attempting to win the Riband. However, as George Behe clarifies, while the *Titanic* was not aiming to set a transatlantic record, she was probably "trying to better the maiden voyage crossing time of her sister ship, the *Olympic*." Don Lynch concurs, stating that, despite the gossip on board, there "was no way the *Titanic* could have captured the Blue Riband." He adds that to beat the current record, held by the Cunard Line's *Mauretania*, the *Titanic* would have had to arrive two whole days ahead of schedule, "and she certainly wasn't capable of that."

That night, as the ship neared the deadly ice zone, Dorothy and her mother dressed for dinner as usual. It's not recorded what Pauline chose to wear for their last meal aboard the *Titanic*, but Dorothy selected her white silk evening dress. "On the night of the disaster there had been a great deal of merriment on board," she would recall in an interview in the *Morning Telegraph* two days following her rescue. In another interview she said dinner that night "was like going to a ball." She attributed the celebratory atmosphere to passengers' anticipation of reaching shore. It's possible, though, that a performance by the band in the lounge that evening had set the stage for the festive attitude and attire of passengers. Word also may have made the rounds that a private supper party, attended by many of the elite, was being held in the restaurant. Whatever the reason, the whole evening was akin to a gala charity affair with men in formal dinner jackets and women wearing their best jewelry and new Paris gowns.

After dinner, Dorothy and Pauline took their nightly stroll before bed. But tonight they were restless and didn't want to turn in early. "Looking back, I believe we were uneasy because of some psychic pull," Dorothy said. As the women circled the promenade deck, they encountered Fred Seward who admitted he wasn't sleepy either and "felt like cards." When Dorothy peevishly reminded her mother and Seward that playing bridge on Sundays was against the rules on White Star ships, they all laughed "as if I had made a delicious joke." They wandered into the ship's library and sat down, ostensibly to read but in truth looking for a fourth partner for bridge. Seated nearby was a handsome, polished young man and Dorothy, bold as ever, walked up to him. Twenty-eight-year-old William Thompson Sloper, a banker from Connecticut, was writing letters to friends, when he noticed "a very pretty woman" approaching. As he explained in his memoirs, the lady frankly introduced herself as well as her shady mission. "Although I was not then, and never have been, a good bridge player, I accepted to join her," he remembered. The quartet headed for the lounge, located forward on A Deck, and commenced their undercover game at about 9:30 p.m. They were still playing almost two hours later when a steward asked them if they would wrap it up so he could turn the lights off.

"We begged to finish the rubber and ordered some Poland water," Dorothy recalled. It was just after 11:30 when the group finally called it a night. Rising to leave, Dorothy tucked into the sash of her gown a box of French matches lying on the table. It would be a fun souvenir of their prohibited game. What a funny story it would make to tell Julie. As they stood in the foyer at the foot of the grand staircase, bathed in a golden glow as most of the lights were turned off, the bunch chatted and laughed over their Sunday night bridge caper. Then Dorothy impulsively invited everyone for a stroll on deck. Her mother and Seward declined but Sloper agreed. While Seward headed to his stateroom, Dorothy went back to her cabin to help her mother undress for bed before rejoining her new friend. Meantime, Sloper returned to his cabin for a coat and hat for their walk. He was on his way back to the foyer when "the ship gave a lurch and seemed to slightly keel over to the left." Dorothy felt the same jar.

"I walked down to my room at 11:40," she would tell the *New York Dramatic Mirror*. "No sooner had I entered my apartment than there suddenly came this long-drawn, sickening scrunch." Her description of the collision with the iceberg was similar when interviewed by *Moving Picture News*; she called it a "peculiar scrunching sound." Dorothy ran back up to A Deck and met Sloper, who had just arrived. Together they rushed out onto the starboard promenade, "supposing that perhaps a propeller had broken, or something of that sort," as Dorothy said. "Peering off into the starlit night," Sloper would write in his book, "we could both of us see something white looming up out of the water and rapidly disappearing off the stern."

Dorothy never forgot the sinister sight. "It was a night to dream of, clear as crystal and brilliant with stars," she said. "Ice was scattered over the deck and there alongside was a huge, shadowy mass." Hearing a passing ship's officer declare that the collision would only "cause a slight delay," she and other passengers, who had been roused by the crash and were congregating on deck, were satisfied that it would amount to little more than a "novel adventure." Still, Dorothy told Sloper she was going below to get her mother. While she was gone, Fred Seward reappeared and joined Sloper at the rail. On her way downstairs, Dorothy passed a steward who refused to answer her question as to the extent of the damage. He tried to push her aside, blurting "Nothing wrong!" as he fled. Once in E-22, she found her mother almost fully dressed, wearing a "coat suit" ensemble – a matching jacket, skirt and overcoat. Pauline, whom Dorothy said would remain "wonderfully calm throughout the ordeal," urged her daughter to change into warmer clothes.

Dorothy said there was no need, and opted for a sweater and polo coat which she tossed over her evening gown. She also grabbed a pair of gloves and a woolen sports cap. Finally, as they left the stateroom, Dorothy kicked off her delicate high-heeled evening shoes and stepped into a pair of sturdier pumps. In their haste, Pauline forgot her gloves. As they entered the E Deck foyer, located near their cabin, the Gibsons noticed water gathering in the stairwell below. Unnerved, the ladies quickly mounted the stairs and joined their bridge mates on the promenade, now crowded with other anxious passengers whom Dorothy recalled "were besieging the bulwarks and asking more questions than one man could answer in a week." Continuing along the outer deck, facing the bow, William Sloper asked his party if they "didn't think we were walking downhill." Dorothy acknowledged she felt the forward list but said her impression was that the ship was also "leaning heavily to one side," the deck being "lopsided," which she later admitted made her feel "somewhat uneasy," though not frightened.

In turning around and heading astern, the foursome again commented about the list, noting that they were now going "uphill." "We both remarked that it did not look right to us," Dorothy remembered of her exchange with Sloper as they strolled along, "and we felt that something must be wrong." Soon Dorothy joined in the chorus of questions being flung at crewmembers whenever they appeared. She decided to ask an officer about the water she had seen below. "One of the compartments has been punctured," he told her, smiling faintly, "but the ship is sturdy enough to weather a little thing like that."

The steward who had broken up her group's card game also passed by and told them all that "the *Titanic* couldn't possibly be sunk." Despite assurances, Dorothy was becoming increasingly worried, particularly after another crewmember made an announcement that all passengers were to don lifejackets and report to the boat deck. She and her group followed the general exodus from the promenade back inside the foyer, which was still only half-lit, and were discussing what to do next when they caught sight of Thomas Andrews, bounding up the grand staircase "three steps at a time." "Dorothy rushed over to him," recounted Sloper, "putting her hands on his arm and demanding to know what had happened. Without answering and with a worried look on his face, he brushed Dorothy aside and continued on up the next flight of steps, presumably on his way to the captain's bridge."

"His face was pallid," she said of Andrews. "When I tried to make further inquiry from him, he simply couldn't speak from his excitement. Then I was frightened." Dorothy claimed in her interview with the *Dramatic Mirror* that she was suddenly so afraid she felt paralyzed. She longed for Julie. Would she see him again? While Sloper and Seward returned to their staterooms, several men assisted the Gibsons into lifejackets, white canvas affairs that tied on the side. One of the men Dorothy recognized to be J. Bruce Ismay, managing director of the White Star Line. He handed the ladies a pair of steamer rugs, directed them upstairs and onto the starboard boat deck. There they found the crew were uncovering the lifeboats and swinging them out in preparation for loading. Standing to the right side of the deck door, mother and daughter were joined once more by their game partners who arrived holding lifejackets. Sloper recalled that the party of four stood for a while in the shelter of a recess on deck while they helped one another adjust their bulky life-saving gear. He noted that, although they spoke to each other, it was hard to hear because of the roar of steam being released from the boilers through the funnels' exhaust valves above.

Among the passengers now crowding onto the boat deck were the Astors, who stood nearby in conversation with several others. Dorothy remembered that they were soon "called away by some message." Dorothy also noticed Thomas Andrews on deck, assisting the crew in preparing the lifeboats for lowering. She said he "ran to and fro with a face of greenish paleness and declined to answer any of the questions hurled at him." It was about 12:30 a.m. now, nearly an hour since the *Titanic*'s collision with the iceberg. The ear-splitting escaping steam had ceased, the sound replaced by soothing, if faint, music from the ship's orchestra which had set up its instruments on the other side of the ship. There was no sign of panic among the other passengers assembling but, as the throng on deck grew and the lifeboats were finally readied, Dorothy began to lose her control.

"I realized we were in great peril," she told the *Morning Telegraph,* "I clung to my mother and pressed my way toward the railing." Sloper recalled the moment in his autobiography. "Every passenger seemed to have taken a firm grip on his nerves," he said. "Dorothy Gibson was the only one to realize the desperate situation we were in because she had become quite hysterical." He remembered that she kept repeating aloud, "I'll never ride in my little gray car again," as she threaded her way through the crush of people toward the lifeboats, anticipating the inevitable order to abandon ship. Pauline followed her daughter, and their two companions followed them. "My mother tells me I was behaving wildly," she said, "and I cannot deny it. I was so afraid. I knew we were going to sink."

It was then that First Officer William Murdoch, placed in charge of the evacuation on the starboard side by Captain Smith, addressed the waiting crowd through a megaphone. "Any passengers who would like to do so may get into this lifeboat," Murdoch called out, motioning to the farthest craft aft, No. 7, which was lowered flush to the deck for taking in passengers. Both Murdoch and Fifth Officer Harold Lowe stood by to help people aboard. Later press reports claimed that Murdoch made a special appeal to the several honeymoon couples present. Helen Bishop, one of these newlyweds, would testify at the American Senate Inquiry into the disaster but did not mention that the first officer singled them out. Even so, she and her husband Dick and another couple, John and Nelle Snyder, standing near, were some of the first passengers to board No. 7.

Dorothy and her party had now made their way through the crowd and approached Murdoch and Lowe. "There was no doubt in Dorothy's mind what she wanted to do," Sloper said. "So with the help of the first officer, I handed Dorothy down into the bow of the lifeboat." While Seward and Lowe assisted Pauline, Dorothy lost her footing due to the motion of the boat as it swung on its davits. "I fell all over myself," she would recall, "as I slid down to the bottom of the boat." Regaining herself, Dorothy reached out to Sloper, still standing on deck. "We won't go unless you do," she said, holding onto his hand, and made an emotional appeal for him to join them. Sloper turned to Seward. "What do you say?" he asked. "What's the difference, we may as well go along," was Seward's reply and the two men jumped in. Sloper would afterwards credit Dorothy's bad nerves and histrionics with saving his life that night.

As there were few others willing to trust themselves to the open boat, the loading went slowly. No one seemed to grasp the urgency of the situation and the officers were having trouble convincing people to quit the ship. Without causing panic by stating the extent of the danger, the men did their best to assure passengers that it was both safe and advisable to leave. Gradually, a trickle of passengers filtered into No. 7 — William Greenfield and his mother Blanche; Alfred Nourney, a 20-year-old German traveling as "Baron von Drachstedt;" three Frenchmen, including sculptor Paul Chevre, aviator Pierre Marechal and merchant Alfred Omont; Lily Potter, her daughter Olive Earnshaw, and a family friend, Margaret Hays, who carried her pet Pomeranian wrapped in a blanket.

These and a dozen others would be the first to escape the *Titanic*. After ten minutes of loading, there were still only twenty-six aboard, of whom fifteen were men, including three crewmembers — lookouts Archie Jewell and George Hogg and seaman William Henry Weller. Murdoch placed Hogg in charge and, though boat 7 had a capacity of sixty-five persons, he ordered it lowered away. Time was wasting, he reasoned; there were nine other lifeboats to attend to manning and lowering. At 12:40 a.m. boat 7, the first to be launched, creaked down its fall lines to the sea, a sobering sixty-foot drop. To add to the terror, the lifeboat's slow descent to the water was very "jerky," Sloper would recall. "That was the most perilous part of the whole adventure," agreed Dorothy in her interview with Chauncey Parsons, "because first one end would drop, then the other. We were absolutely silent until we reached the waves."

As boat 7 touched the water, Murdoch yelled down his last instructions to its crew: "Stand by and return when we call you." Lookout Jewell testified at the British Board of Trade Inquiry into the sinking that as there was an open gangway door on D Deck, he assumed they might be asked to row over to it at some point to take on more passengers. Lookout Hogg, assisted by Jewell and Weller, ordered the ropes freed. He then divided a stack of steamer rugs among the women and assigned oars to his mates as well as to some of the passengers, including Sloper and Pierre Marechal. Alfred Nourney was asked to row but refused; instead he lit a cigar. Hogg ignored him and asked one of the women to steer. At last, the lifeboat pushed off from the ship's side, turning its bow into the night. The boat was some yards away, floating astern, when suddenly, as if to underscore the urgency of the moment, a deafening clamor came from the bridge area of the *Titanic* as the first of a series of distress rockets exploded, searing the calm night air. The unreality of watching the detonation of a rocket overhead while afloat in a small boat could not have aided Dorothy's failing nerves. As No. 7 rowed into the darkness, she couldn't believe what was happening.

Trouble arose almost immediately. Several passengers shouted that there was water collecting in the bottom of the boat, the drainage plug having been accidentally kicked out. It was replaced and some of the water absorbed by what Dorothy called "volunteer contributions of lingerie from the women and garments from the men." But most of the water

HANDS ACROSS THE SEA

continued sloshing at people's feet, soiling coat and skirt hems, even muddying the train of Dorothy's new white dress. She told a reporter after her rescue that the boat's plug didn't fit and "someone had to sit on it all the time to keep it down."

Splashing away from the dying *Titanic*, No. 7 drifted against the macabre sound of music in the distance, interrupted at intervals by the jolting blast of the rockets. Wet with perspiration from rowing, Sloper gave his overcoat to Dorothy to wear, and she "thanked him with a kiss." Her own sweater and short coat were not enough protection from the cold, she found. "I never knew one could be so cold and live," she said. "I ached from head to foot, and I was much more warmly clad than some of the women." Pierre Marechal, finding himself in the same shape as Sloper as he tugged at his oar, loaned his coat, jacket and gloves to the thinly dressed women around him. Witnessing his largesse, Dorothy said Marechal "was simply splendid," although she was amused he "managed to wear his monocle throughout the excitement." According to Jewell's testimony, Hogg ordered the boat halted at about twenty yards. There it remained for more than an hour, its passengers watching the lowering of the other lifeboats, their departure, the crowds either lining the rails or moving aft, and the beautiful ship sagging lower into the deep, her stern slowly rising. "The sea was perfectly calm," said Sloper. "Not even a ripple on the surface. For the next hour and a half we just sat there."

Boat 7's long vigil had begun. Dorothy and Pauline, huddling together, refused to believe their eyes. "As soon as we were at a safe distance from the *Titanic*," Dorothy explained, "we turned to watch the great liner settling gradually down into the water. It was like a nightmare." From their vantage point so near the ship, Dorothy and the others in boat 7 could easily observe the evacuation. "We could hear the murmur of voices and now and then the shouting of officers," Dorothy said. One by one, they saw the other lifeboats launched and rowed swiftly away. But as the last boat cut loose from the ship, Dorothy could still see hundreds of people on deck. Hogg didn't want to move his boat from the position he had been ordered to take, but by 2 a.m. it was obvious the end was near for the ship and those who remained aboard. Murdoch's call to return would not come, he thought. The *Titanic*'s bow was now completely underwater, the stern with its massive, dripping propellers exposed.

For the safety of his boat Hogg reluctantly ordered No. 7 rowed clear. Jewell later claimed at the inquiry in London that their boat was the last one standing by. For almost the whole of the sinking, it had hovered near in hopes of rendering aid. But there was nothing that could be done now that wouldn't endanger the lives of its occupants. And so the little boat moved farther out into the starry night, its oars swishing in the inky sea, all eyes aboard glued to the *Titanic*. The ship was ominously silent, Dorothy remembered, adding that the whole scene was enveloped in an "unnatural calmness." There were no more distress rockets firing, no more music playing. "Suddenly there was a wild coming together of voices from the ship," recalled Dorothy, "and we noticed an unusual commotion among the people about the railing. Then the awful thing happened, the thing that will remain in my memory until the day I die." The *Titanic*'s stern swung up rapidly while her bow dug into the waves. Cries pierced the air and there were thunderous crashes from deep in the ship. Then the lights failed, plunging all into darkness. As Sloper would write: "The ship remained until two or three minutes before she sank as brilliantly lighted as she was directly after the accident. Then suddenly, just like in a theatre before the curtain goes up, all the lights dipped simultaneously to a pale glow."

Dorothy also recalled that the lights didn't go out at once. "The lights flickered out," she said. "Then with a lurch the *Titanic* slid forward." In the darkness, Dorothy could not make out clearly what was happening to the ship, which was now but a shadow angled against the stars. Her description, however, indicates she saw the stern settle back during the *Titanic*'s splitting apart at the keel, just aft of amidships. "A pause of silence held everyone spellbound," she remembered, "until the stern shot back into sight. A minute later she swayed and disappeared." Again, Sloper's account is similar: "A moment or two later everyone saw, silhouetted against the starlit sky, the stern rising perpendicularly into the air. Then with a prolonged rush and roar, the great ship went down."

It was 2:20 a.m., two hours and 40 minutes after the *Titanic* had suffered its death wound. But the worst had only begun for the hundreds of men, women and children on the *Titanic*, as they were tossed into the freezing sea. Their cries resounded like a cathedral's haunting echo across the water. Dorothy was in shock as she listened. "There burst out the most ghastly cries, shrieks, yells and moans that a mortal could ever imagine," she told the *Dramatic Mirror*. She also recounted the horror of the sinking to the *New York Telegraph*: "The concerted cry of despair is ringing in my ears this minute," she said. "It seemed like a mighty wail, commingling the hoarse shouts of the men and the shrill screams of the women." Another sound was almost as frightening. Although the *Titanic* had disappeared, terrible explosions could be heard, coming from underwater; to Dorothy it was a "rumble like Niagra." The sunken stern, now falling away many feet below the surface, had imploded.

Heeding the cries of the dying, Lookout Hogg suggested that boat 7 return to rescue swimmers. In almost a unison response, his scared passengers discouraged him. Dorothy, in relating this episode, did not record her feelings about turning back, perhaps out of guilt, for surely she was among those protesting. Self-preservation in moments of extreme danger may be innate human mechanisms but they seem cowardly when examined from the perspective of calm and safety. With people going to their deaths only a few hundred yards away, Dorothy felt helpless and sickened. From the time she had first seen the grand ship, nestled in the bay at Cherbourg in the honeyed glow of early evening, until tonight's unholy scenes, it seemed as if the world had changed. "It was a sense of desolation never to be forgotten," Dorothy said.

The feeling was compounded by the total darkness that enshrouded the little fleet of lifeboats the *Titanic* left behind. The situation concerned Lookout Hogg, who announced that as their boat was without a lantern or a compass, it might be a good idea to have some matches handy should a signal be required. Dorothy remembered the souvenir matchbox from her card game. It was still tucked into her belt. She handed it to Hogg but the matches were never used, she said. With the cries of drowning people filling the ears of its occupants, boat 7 drifted. "No one in the boat said a word," Dorothy remembered. "There was nothing to say and nothing we could do." Dorothy's thoughts turned to her lover, safe at home, unaware of the tragedy she was facing. How worried Julie would be when he learned what had happened. She could not then have guessed the extent to which he would go in order to reach her once he discovered her peril. Suddenly Dorothy noticed boat 7 was floating near several other lifeboats. The sailors manning them were calling back and forth to each other. Toward dawn, as the calls from the dying faded, a breeze sprang up.

"It whipped the sea into waves and chilled us through and through," Dorothy said. She shivered under a rug with her mother, trying to escape the freezing wind. Lifeboat No. 5, with Third Officer Herbert Pitman in charge, soon drew near and as it carried more than forty passengers, he ordered some of them transferred to boat 7 to lessen his own boat's weight in the choppy waters. Among the people joining No. 7 were Ruth Dodge and her 5-year-old son, Washington. The two lifeboats were eventually lashed together so as to be more visible to possible rescuers the next morning. Despite the cold and the increase of danger brought by the threat of heavy seas, "everybody was cheerful in his suffering," Dorothy recalled. Only one "chap," she said, revealed himself as less than heroic. Alfred Nourney, who had refused to take an oar, was oblivious to his plight. Dorothy and Pauline watched in astonishment as he "gathered all the blankets to himself" and "calmly stretched himself out in the forepart of the lifeboat" where he "promptly fell asleep regardless of what might happen." Meanwhile, green flares fired from another lifeboat, No. 2, under the command of Fourth Officer Joseph Boxhall, alternately encouraged and confused those in the other boats. Dorothy recalled that although each flare saw passengers in boat 7 "jumping up at every false alarm of a ship in sight," the lights kept everyone's morale up.

"Just when our spirits sagged, there would be another light which gave us courage again," she said. "I will not forget those little lights of hope in the dark." Gradually conversation resumed among the occupants of No. 7, bringing them out of what Dorothy termed their "miserable agony." Sloper asked Dorothy what would be the first thing she would do if she were saved. "I will thank the Lord," she replied. The two also talked of the loss of life, which Dorothy believed must be slight until a crewman interrupted and "told us that if the boats were filled, not more than a third of those on the *Titanic* could have escaped." They then discussed whether the ship's wireless operator "had stuck to his post" and managed to contact any steamers in the vicinity with a "C.Q.D." (the regulation distress code). They would soon have ample proof that the *Titanic*'s radio operators, Harold Bride and Jack Phillips, had indeed fulfilled their duty. By 4 a.m. as dawn broke over the frigid North Atlantic, a row of lights and a cloud of smoke could be seen on the horizon. "We watched that streak of black smoke grow larger and larger," Dorothy said, "and then we were able to discern the hull of a ship heading in our direction." Someone shouted that the approaching vessel was "crowding on all steam," which sent a note of cheer through the boat. For Dorothy, the ship coming their way was her release from terror. She knew she would be saved and that she would see Julie again.

"It's all right now, ladies," Lookout Hogg called out. "Do not grieve. We are picked up!" The ship racing to their rescue was the Cunard Line's *Carpathia*. Commanded by Captain Arthur Rostron, the *Carpathia* had been en route to the Mediterranean when her wireless man received the *Titanic*'s emergency call. Through an ice-strewn sea, the ship had dashed fifty eight miles. "Never was I so glad of anything in my life," Dorothy would relate, "as when the blessed *Carpathia* appeared in the distance. With numb hands we rowed towards her." Boats 7 and 5 untied but kept close together as they made their way through the rough sea and surrounding ice. As they rowed, Dorothy noticed a grim sight – the green sofa cushions from the *Titanic*'s lounge were bobbing in the water nearby. Was this all that was left of the majestic ship?

The sad but beautiful dawn of April 15 was in full glory as the *Titanic*'s lifeboats drew alongside the rescue ship. "It took us an hour to awkwardly row our boat to the side of the *Carpathia*," recalled Sloper. "During that hour the sun came out of the ocean like a ball of fire. Its rays reflected on the numerous icebergs sticking up out of the sea around us." The minute No. 7 glided under a gangway door of the ship, rope ladders and slings were lowered to hoist its occupants on deck. The lifeboat was the third to reach the *Carpathia*, preceded by boats 2 and 1. Boat 5 followed closely behind. As the unloading began, Dorothy looked up at the ship "with its rails swarming with kindly faces, crowding about in the anxiety to render help." The disembarkation of passengers from the boats was achieved without major incident. Men and the more agile of the women clambered up the ladders while most other women and children seated themselves in chair slings that were raised slowly up the side; some of the kids were even plopped into canvas bags and hauled aloft.

Once aboard, the *Carpathia*'s stewards and stewardesses took charge of the survivors, offering them breakfast, coffee and blankets. Dorothy, standing on deck in her bedraggled evening dress, was approached by two *Carpathia* passengers, James Russell Lowell and his wife, who invited her to share their cabin. Pauline was also provided a berth in a cabin. The outpouring of sympathy from the crew and passengers was overwhelming to mother and daughter. "Captain Rostron had caused everything to be placed in readiness," Dorothy told the *Morning Telegraph*, "and as the accommodations were limited, the passengers opened their staterooms and did everything in their power to allay our suffering." To *Moving Picture News* she also praised the *Carpathia*'s people. "Everyone was so perfectly splendid to us," she said. "The women aboard all came and offered us their berths and clothes and in fact anything that they had of which we could make use." After the *Carpathia* had taken aboard all survivors from the lifeboats — only 712 out of the 2,208 who had set sail on the *Titanic* five days earlier — the Cunarder cruised slowly over the grave of the lost ship, searching for life along miles of scattered debris.

Finding but one body, which was recovered, Captain Rostron was satisfied he had done "all that could be done." At 8:50 a.m. the *Carpathia* turned sorrowfully back for New York. The voyage home was one of grief and reflection for the survivors. Dorothy and Pauline had lost no loved ones, but despaired for those of their fellow passengers who had. Moreover, like everyone else, they were in shock that such a catastrophe could have occurred. They tried to console their friends and acquaintances while accepting the generosity of their saviors. One of their fellow passengers disgusted them, however. Alfred Nourney, the arrogant "baron," who had refused to row in boat 7, choosing to sleep instead, made yet more enemies once aboard the *Carpathia*. The Gibsons, Helen Bishop and others from No. 7 were in the dining saloon, which was being used as a dormitory, when they saw Nourney helping himself to a pallet of blankets. As Dorothy later claimed, the man "appropriated no less than forty five blankets to make himself a soft bed." Bishop and another passenger, Elmer Taylor, recalled that the whole room plunged into laughter and applause when a young woman (possibly Canadian Alice Fortune) approached Nourney's little nest and pulled the bottom layer of blankets out from under him, sending him flailing across the floor. In addition to being given staterooms, while so many others slept on floors in the ship's public rooms, the Gibsons were fortunate in being provided changes of clothing, which enabled Dorothy to return Sloper's overcoat.

"I won't forget what you did for me," she told him as she handed it back to him on deck. "And I won't forget what you did for me," Sloper said and the two embraced ("like silly kids," as Dorothy said).

"I was so tired I slept twenty six hours after getting on board the *Carpathia*," Dorothy claimed. Pauline, similarly exhausted from their experience, rested in her cabin for most of the day. Little else is known about the Gibsons' experiences on the rescue ship's voyage to New York, which Dorothy characterized as "three days of suspense." The women spoke with others of their fellow passengers and heard their stories of escape. Some of what they were told was sensational and unsubstantiated but, for Dorothy, a common thread ran through the accounts she heard – a lack of discipline among the *Titanic*'s officers and crew. Still emotional, she allowed these tales to influence her and, although she didn't personally witness any examples of cowardice or ill-judgment on the part of the crew, she would speak vehemently against them to the press on her arrival in New York. Sloper, by whose side she remained throughout the ordeal, didn't agree with Dorothy's view of the crew at all. His impression was that the sailors "knew their business" and handled the evacuation "skill-fully."

By the afternoon of April 17, Dorothy was frantic to send a wireless message to Julie to assure him of her safety. But the line was long at the Marconi office. She would have to wait. Finally a message came through from Julie — a heartrending cry from home: "Will be worried to death till I hear from you, what awful agony, Julie." Back in New York, desperate for news from Dorothy, Brulatour wasn't waiting around. In cooperation with William Randolph Hearst's *New York American*, Julie chartered an ocean-going tug, the *Mary Scully*. A filmmaker through and through, the head of Kodak loaded it with cameras and photographers; only decorum prevented Julie's boarding the boat himself. His newsreel crew, along with one special passenger, wireless hero Jack Binns (who had sent out the first recorded "SOS" during the 1908 *Republic* sinking), was aiming full speed for the scene of the disaster when it received word that the *Carpathia* was nearing New York with the only survivors found. The *Mary Scully* reversed course and headed to meet the *Carpathia*. Finally on Thursday, April 18, the day of the *Carpathia*'s scheduled arrival in New York, Dorothy's cable (only a brief one, as she had to borrow money to pay for it) was sent to Julie: "Safe, picked up by *Carpathia*, don't worry, Dorothy."

Thrilled to know she was alive, Julie looked forward to their pre-arranged appoint-ment. In the late evening of April 18, nothing less dramatic than a thunderstorm would do for the *Carpathia*'s entry into New York Harbor. Carrying its pitifully meager contingent of *Titanic* survivors, the vessel passed the Statue of Liberty, Ellis Island and the Battery, on its way to Pier 54. Ahead, an estimated 50,000 people crammed the shores to see the rescue ship dock. Out of the mist came the lights of a small craft. It was the *Mary Scully*, the tug Julie had chartered, the first of a swarm of boats, each hired by competing New York dailies, to converge on the scene. As the rescue ship edged into the harbor, *Carpathia* and *Titanic* passengers lined the rails, meeting the stares of huddled, rain-soaked clusters of people in the dark. All the while, the press boats swirled around the ship, reporters yelling questions at the silent crowd on deck.

For the time being, Dorothy was among that wordless throng. But after stepping ashore and into the arms of her family and friends, she found the courage to express herself through a medium available to no one else who had survived the *Titanic*. For an actress to parlay her experiences into a staged production may have been a natural impulse, as she would later claim, but the decision was also unquestionably prompted by her producers' savvy marketing strategy. Some would criticize her foray into a cinematic recreation of the *Titanic* disaster, but in Dorothy's mind to relive her ordeal before audiences was to give validation to the public's grief, which needed a vent. "The nation and the world had been profoundly grieved by the sinking of the *Titanic*," she said many years later, "and I had the opportunity to pay tribute to those who gave their lives on that awful night. That is all I tried to do."

Eclair's presentation of *Saved From the Titanic,* released less than a month after Dorothy's rescue, would not only depict an extraordinary moment in history, enacted by an actual participant in the original event, but it would redefine the actress's identity as a woman. The public's image of Dorothy, the model and movie star, would be fused with the stark reality of Dorothy, the *Titanic* survivor. Even after her professional fame had passed, it was the real-life, off-screen role she played in an unthinkable disaster that would assure immortality for Dorothy Gibson.

Chapter 6:
A Living Memory
1912

THROUGH THE LIGHTNING and rain that greeted the *Carpathia*'s arrival in New York, Dorothy and Pauline, standing at the railing, took in the surreal scene. Among the hopeful masses along the pier, they caught sight of friends and relatives. As the *Carpathia* made its berth, there were no whistle blasts or cheering crowds as would customarily attend a ship's arrival. Only silence.After the gangplank had been lowered and her turn came in the queue of disembarking survivors, Dorothy remembered she "ran crying down the ramp" into the outstretched arms of her father, Leonard Gibson, himself "laboring under strain to contain his emotions." Others welcoming mother and daughter home were Pauline's sister, Mrs. A.W. Todd, several of Pauline's neighbors and old church friends from Hoboken, Dorothy's agent Pat Casey and her co-star Muriel Ostriche. Leonard led his family past the throng of spectators, including a horde of newsreel photographers, some of whom were probably from Julie's *Animated Weekly*. When a teenage porter approached them on their way from the wharf to a taxi, offering to help with baggage, Pauline sobbed that they had saved nothing. Leonard tipped the boy anyway, telling him, "But they are saved, my child. Praise God!"

Dorothy wasn't disappointed to find that Julie wasn't at the dock to greet her. She knew he was discreetly awaiting their private reunion. After bidding goodnight to her parents at a party her father had arranged at a hotel restaurant, she rushed back to her apartment to prepare to join Julie. Dolling up without the alluring aid of her Parisian lingerie, she made the best of clothes Muriel had loaned and laid out for her. Dorothy was ecstatic as she jumped into the little gray car she thought she would never drive again. The moment she had dreamt of was at hand. Racing through the wet streets of New York City, anticipating their first embrace after a month apart, Dorothy realized how much more meaningful her long-awaited rendezvous with Julie would be now that death had threatened to separate them. The lovers' midnight consummation, with its caresses and tearful kisses, and the rain at the windows, became one of her sweetest memories.

Dorothy's few passionate hours with Julie — during which, as she told Muriel, he presented her with a $1,000 diamond "engagement" ring — were her last moments of peace before

Dorothy Gibson in one of her first
publicity photos as leading lady for
the Eclair Film Company, 1911.

Harrison Fisher's "Down the
Avenue," depicting
Dorothy Gibson, 1910.

Dorothy Winifred Brown, age two.
Courtesy: Marsha Buckley

Pauline Boeson Brown Gibson.
Courtesy: Phillip Gowan

Dorothy (far left), performing as Polly Stanley, in *The Lady From Lane's*, 1907.
Courtesy: Victoria Alvarez

Dorothy (center) in Charles Frohman's *The Dairymaids,* 1907.

Charles Frohman

Harrison Fisher

"Roses" by Harrison Fisher, posed by Dorothy Gibson, 1909. This was one of
Dorothy's first sittings for the famous commercial artist

Untitled illustration by Harrison Fisher, posed by Dorothy Gibson, 1911.

"My Queen," by Fisher, posed by Dorothy, 1910.

Fisher's "Music Hath Charms," posed by Dorothy, 1910.

Dorothy, 1911.

Harrison Fisher's "Mary," depicting
Dorothy Gibson, appeared on
the cover of the April 8, 1911 issue of
The Saturday Evening Post.

July

15 Cents

COSMOPOLITAN

Portraying Dorothy, "Bows Attract Beaus"
by Fisher was featured on the cover
of *Cosmopolitan*, July 1911.

This 1911 cameo portrait of Dorothy Gibson was widely published, appearing
in *Billboard*, the *Dramatic Mirror*, *Moving Picture World* and the *Morning Telegraph*.

Another extensively reproduced publicity photo of Dorothy, 1911.

Fisher's "Refreshments," used for the
June 1911 cover of *Cosmopolitan*,
portrayed Dorothy as a blonde.

"The Trousseau," by Fisher utilized Dorothy's image for all four subjects, 1910.

Untitled Harrison Fisher illustration featuring Dorothy Gibson, 1910.

Fisher's "My Lady Drives"
portraying Dorothy, 1910.

Untitled Fisher image of
Dorothy, 1911.

Before joining Eclair, Dorothy Gibson appeared briefly in Lubin Films. She is seen here (seated) in a scene from the western drama *Good for Evil,* released July 15, 1911.

Eclair

ADOPTS A NEW TRADE MARK AND MAKES AN IMPORTANT STATEMENT:

AMERICAN ECLAIRS will hereafter be designated by "FAME". Titles and sub-titles will carry the new decoration. The Theme itself will be ECLAIR'S Guiding Spirit in the future.

THESE AMERICAN ECLAIRS will be regularly issued on TUESDAY (Drama) and THURSDAY (Comedy) supplemented by photos in sets and improved lithographs for lobby display. Photos supplied to exchanges one week in advance of release date, without charge.

THE PARIS-AMERICANIZED ECLAIR will be issued on SUNDAY, beginning February 18th, and will embody TWO subjects on one reel. Titles and sub-titles written in America. Posters only furnished.

VALUABLE ILLUSTRATED BOOK SENT FREE to those not now on the ECLAIR mammoth mailing list. Send for one today.

EUROPEAN STUDIO: **ECLAIR** AMERICAN STUDIO:
PARIS, FRANCE **FILM CO.** FORT LEE, N. J.

SALES COMPANY SOLE AGENTS

A 1912 Eclair Film Company advertisement from *Moving Picture World..*

Screen captures from Dorothy Gibson's only surviving film, *The Lucky Holdup*, released April 11, 1912.

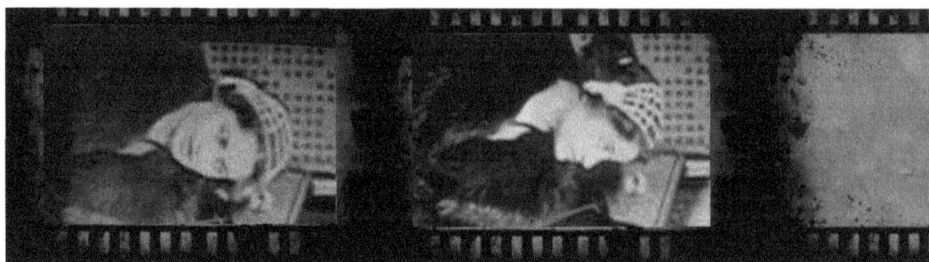

MOVING PICTURE NEWS

Volume IV
No. 46

November 18
1911

PRICE
TEN
CENTS

Scene from
"Hands Across the Sea in '76"
ECLAIR Release of November 21st

Dorothy (center) in the French Court scene from *Hands Across the Sea*, 1911.

Scene of a war widow, played by Dorothy, grieving over her husband's grave in *Hands Across the Sea.*

December 1911 advertisement for *Hands Across the Sea* in which Dorothy received her first star billing.

Illustration by Percy Moran of Dorothy portraying heroine Molly Pitcher in *Hands Across the Sea.*

In a scene from *Hands Across the Sea* Dorothy played a maiden rescued by George Washington from the threat of rape.

Dorothy Gibson (left) with costar Helen Marten in a scene from *Hands Across the Sea.*

The director, crew and cast for the 1912 Eclair drama, *The Awakening.* Seated are Bill Haddock (reading script) and Georges Benot. Standing (from left) are Lucien Andriot, Guy Oliver, Florence Hale, Lamar Johnstone, Dorothy Gibson, Rolinda Bainbridge, Darwin Karr and Louis Grisel. *Courtesy: Marc Wanamaker/Bison Archives.*

Photo feature from
Billboard magazine, 1911.

February 1912 Eclair publicity photo. Seated is Georges Benot. Standing (from left) are Lucien
Andriot, Guy Oliver, Dorothy Gibson, Lamar Johnstone, Florence Hale, Rolinda Bainbridge,
Bill Haddock, Louis Grisel and Darwin Karr. *Courtesy: Marc Wanamaker/Bison Archives*

Promotional photo of Dorothy from the *Dramatic Mirror*, 1911.

COMING!

Tuesday, Jan. 23

*A Delightful Comedy
by Blanch Schreck*

Love Finds A Way

Copyright 1912 by Eclair

With DOROTHY GIBSON and a
·strong supporting cast.

— * —

Thursday, Jan. 25

Another Comedy
WANTED, A GOVERNESS
and on the same reel

THE TURKISH POLICE
a page from Oriental·Life.

Moving Picture World ad for *Love Finds a Way*, one of Dorothy's most popular comedies for Eclair, 1912.

Jules Brulatour, 1911.

Dorothy, 1911.

Eclair Film Company ad for the studio's March 1912 releases.

Divorcons, starring Dorothy and Jack Adolfi (on right). Released January 2, 1912.

Mamie Bolton starring Dorothy (right). The other players include
Julia Stuart, Alec B. Francis and Darwin Karr. Released January 16, 1912.

Dorothy (left) in another comedic action shot from *Mamie Bolton*, with
Lamar Johnstone and Julia Stuart.

The Guardian Angel, directed by Etienne Arnaud, and starring Dorothy and Lamar Johnstone. Released February 27, 1912.

Dorothy (seated, left) in *Getting Dad Married.* One of her costars was Jack Adolfi (far right). Released February 29, 1912.

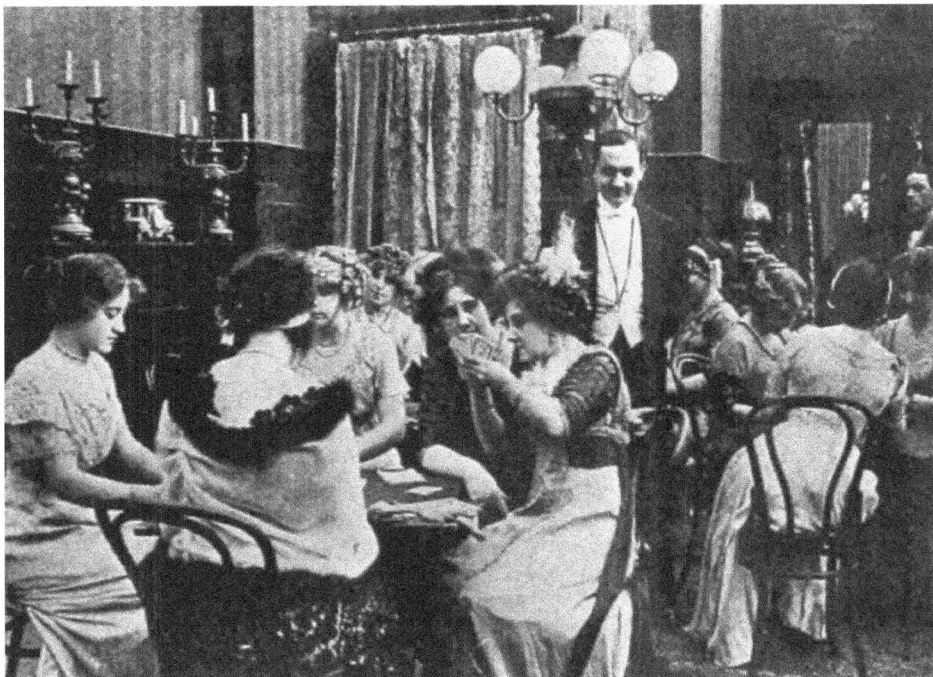

Bridge, starring Dorothy (far left). Her co-star was Jack Adolfi (center).
Released March 12, 1912.

Another scene from *Bridge*, starring Dorothy (seated foreground, second from left).

It Pays to be KInd, featuring (from left) Dorothy, Julia Stuart, Isabel Lamon and Rolinda Bainbridge. Released March 19, 1912.

Another scene from *It Pays to be Kind*, featuring Dorothy (far left). Guy Oliver (right) was the male lead in this film. Lamar Johnstone (background) played a butler.

Dorothy in an episode of *The Revenge of the Silk Masks,* an early serial.
Released April 30, 1912.

The Revenge of the Silk Masks, starring Dorothy (center). Her costars included Muriel Ostriche
(in foreground) and Alec Francis (second from right).

Dorothy Gibson (right) and Julia Stuart in *The Easter Bonnet*.
Released April 25, 1912. *Courtesy: Frank Thompson*

Dorothy (foreground center) in another scene from *The Easter Bonnet*. Her costars included Jack Adolfi (left) and Muriel Ostrich (seated).

A screen capture from Dorothy's only known surviving film, *The Lucky Holdup,* co-starring Lamar Johnstone. Released April 11, 1912. *Courtesy: Jennifer Mills*

On April 10, 1912, Dorothy and Pauline Gibson sailed aboard
the *Titanic* and onto the pages of history. *Courtesy: George Behe*

When the *Titanic* left Europe on its maiden voyage to New York, the ship
carried more than 2,200 passengers and crew. *Courtesy: George Behe*

Thomas Andrews, the *Titanic*'s builder, was one of Dorothy's table companions.

Dorothy and her mother survived the *Titanic*'s sinking in Lifeboat No. 7, the first to leave the ship.

The rescue of the *Titanic*'s survivors by the *Carpathia* was recorded by one of its passengers, painter Colin Campbell Cooper. *Courtesy: Butterfield, Butterfield and Dunning*

Jules Brulatour's "Titanic Wreck" newsreel, issue No. 7 of the *Animated Weekly,* was presented to overflow crowds at movie houses across the country.

Advertisement for *Saved From the Titanic* from *Moving Picture World*. Although the
release date here is cited as May 14 it was delayed in production by two days.

A telegram Jules Brulatour sent to Dorothy Gibson aboard the *Titanic*, dated April 12. It reads: "Will do everything make you completely happy. Love you madly, Julie."

Dorothy in the finale of *Saved From the Titanic*, in which her father, played by Alec Francis (left), gives his consent for her to marry her sweetheart, Ensign Jack, portrayed by Jack Adolfi. Released May 16, 1912.

A promotional photo for *Saved From the Titanic,* showing Dorothy Gibson wearing the same sweater she wore the night she escaped the sinking ship.

Scene from *Saved From the Titanic* in which Dorothy relates her experiences in the disaster to costars Alec Francis, Jack Adolfi and Julia Stuart.

Another promotional shot for *Saved From the Titanic,* showing
Dorothy pointing on a map to the location of her nightmare experience.
Courtesy: Frank Thompson

Dorothy in her last publicity photo for Eclair Films. This portrait was used to promote the release of *Saved From the Titanic* in England and France in the summer of 1912.

One of the last Harrison Fisher images of Dorothy was this cover illustration for the
Ladies' Home Journal, June 1912.

Art Model to Wed Midas
He Needs Divorce First

MISS DOROTHY GIBSON.

When Dorothy Gibson's affair with Jules Brulatour
was exposed in 1913, the scandal was
nationwide news.

This impromptu photo of famous movie stars and directors was taken on the World Film Company
lot in 1915. Why Dorothy (seated right) was in the picture is unknown as she was then retired from
film work. She is joined by actors Wilton Lackaye (seated center), Elaine Hammerstein (seated left),
Holbrook Blinn (standing behind Lackaye), Alice Brady (third from right) and Clara Kimball Young
(far right). Director Maurice Tourneur is standing at center back.

Jules Brulatour (fifth from left) with fellow members of the executive committee of the Motion Picture Board of Trade in 1915.

Dorothy Gibson Brulatour, 1920.
Courtesy: Phillip Gowan

The flirtatious character of Dorothy (center) in Anita Loos' 1925 comedic novel *Gentlemen Prefer Blondes* was probably based on Dorothy Gibson Brulatour.

Dorothy Brulatour, 1930.
Courtesy: Phillip Gowan

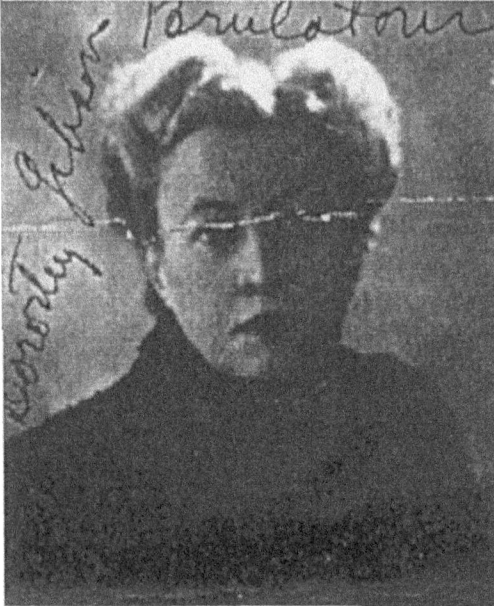

Dorothy's 1944 passport photo.
Courtesy: Phillip Gowan

Indro Montanelli

Nicholas Franco (center), brother of Spain's dictator, with Dorothy's lover Antonio Ramos (just behind Franco), at the Nazi Party Congress in 1937.

EVERYBODY'S TALKING ABOUT IT!

It's Terrific!

ORSON WELLES

CITIZEN KANE

The Mercury Actors

JOSEPH COTTEN
DOROTHY COMINGORE
EVERETT SLOANE
RAY COLLINS
GEORGE COULOURIS
AGNES MOOREHEAD
PAUL STEWART
RUTH WARRICK
ERSKINE SANFORD
WILLIAM ALLAND

The character of Susan Alexander in 1941's *Citizen Kane* was partly based on Dorothy Gibson.

Dorothy in one of her
last photographs, 1945.
Courtesy: Phillip Gowan

Father Giovanni Barbareschi who
schemed to smuggle Dorothy out of
Milan's San Vittore prison in 1944.
Courtesy: Giovanni Barbareschi

Firma del Titolare

Roberto Rossellini's 1959 film *General Della Rovere* was based on Indro Montanelli's book about his escape with Dorothy from the Nazis in 1944.

Barbareschi and Montanelli were reunited 60 years after their flight with Dorothy from San Vittore. *Courtesy: Giovanni Barbaerschi*

Dorothy Gibson Brulatour is buried with her mother in the civilian section of Saint Germain-en-Laye Cemetery near Paris. *Courtesy: Robert Rydell Shotton*

The former First Baptist Church of Hoboken, where Dorothy was baptized, as it looks today. *Courtesy: Jonathan Whitney*

The White Star Line tender *Nomadic*, which ferried Dorothy out to the *Titanic* 100 years ago, has been restored and is now permanently moored at Belfast, Northern Ireland, where it was built. *Courtesy: Robert Rydell Shotton*

Sophie Winkleman portrayed Dorothy Gibson in the 2012 British miniseries *Titanic,* commemorating the centenary of the shipwreck. *Courtesy: ITV*

Sophie Winkleman (left) as Dorothy and Sally Bankes as Pauline in the miniseries *Titanic* in 2012. *Courtesy: ITV*

FINDING DOROTHY

being bombarded by the press about the *Titanic*. She had also agreed to a request from Julie and other Éclair producers to appear in a new movie based on her experiences, and she would have to report to work in the studio almost immediately. The round of interviews with journalists and the beginning of filming were grueling for Dorothy but she held up to the pressure. Perhaps she had the willpower to forge ahead because she intended the *Titanic* picture to be her last, regardless of whether Éclair had found a suitable replacement for her. Whatever the source of her strength, in a matter of days she spoke to representatives for most of the theatrical media — *Billboard, Variety, Moving Picture News*, the *Moving Picture World* and the *New York Dramatic Mirror*, as well as daily newspapers like the *New York Sun* and the *Morning Telegraph*. It was to the latter publication that Dorothy granted her first interview. The reporter who met her the day after her rescue detected she had "suffered from exposure," and described her mood as "at once reminiscently sorrowful and dispassionately calm." She may also have still been in shock. "It seems almost impossible," she told the *Morning Telegraph*, "in the brief time since we left the other side that this great steamship lies at the bottom of the ocean."

Several publications for which she was not personally interviewed carried stories of her escape — the *New York Herald* and the *Tribune* among them; even the conservative *New York Times* featured a portrait of the rescued star on the front page of its April 17 issue. One of her first interviews in the weekly film press was with *Moving Picture News,* which featured her story on April 27. When she met with the reporter for the magazine, Dorothy was still wearing the shoes she had on when she abandoned ship. "When I went to my stateroom," she told the *News*, "I had light satin slippers on, and when I came up I had on these black pumps that you see on me now, but I do not know when or how I got them on."

In some of these published accounts, Dorothy revealed her near-contempt for the crew of the *Titanic*, claiming the men were "slipshod in the extreme." In the *Morning Telegraph* of April 21 she did not mince words:

> *Once aboard the* Carpathia, *it became evident to me that there had been a deplorable lack of discipline on board the* Titanic. *Comparison of the two crews brought this truth home to me. In the exciting moments before the sinking of the* Titanic, *there appeared no concerted action among the officers and crew. Everything was confusion.... I am thankful that my mother and the others, as well as myself, were rescued and that we are back in New York. But it is my sincere wish that the officials of the White Star Line be made to answer for the negligence that caused this disaster, and the pain and sorrow they have brought upon the survivors. The 'unsinkable'* Titanic *might still be the monarch of the sea had ordinary precaution been used in charting her course and providing a sufficient number of lifeboats.*

She was equally forthright in an article appearing in the May 1 edition of the *New York Dramatic Mirror:*

> *The discipline of the crew was wretched for no one knew what to do.... A panic broke out on the* Titanic *after the first boats left, and men had been shot to keep*

67

A LIVING MEMORY

them from filling the remaining boats. The steerage had broken loose and swept things before them. The women who were saved after that owe their lives to the sublime heroism of the men among the passengers. The officers were powerless to control the crew. A steward told me that if the crew had realized sooner the fate before them, few passengers would have been saved.

Dorothy's statements about the crew's behavior during the sinking were largely based on somewhat exaggerated stories related to her on the rescue ship by fellow survivors. As her lifeboat was the first to leave, she could not have directly known what occurred aboard the *Titanic* after her departure. Dorothy's vehemence toward the crew reflects her understandably high state of emotion in the aftermath of the disaster but her criticism of the navigation of the ship — steaming full speed through a sea of ice — and the inadequate equipage of lifeboats seems more than just.

Her ire at this time may also have been roused by knowledge of the ill treatment that her friend, William Sloper, was suffering in certain sectors of the press. After leaving the *Carpathia*, Sloper was followed by journalists to his hotel. However, in announcing that he was giving an exclusive interview to his hometown newspaper, he offended an unscrupulous reporter for the *New York Evening Journal* who concocted as revenge the devastating story of Sloper's escaping the *Titanic* in women's clothes. This report was syndicated and thereafter picked up by the tabloids, doing much harm to Sloper's reputation. Discouraged by his family from filing a lawsuit, he rode out the controversy, which is still one of the *Titanic*'s most enduring legends. Dorothy's other bridge companion from the *Titanic*, Fred Seward, was also facing the media full-force at this time. He had formed a committee of survivors to recognize the valor of Captain Rostron and on May 29, before news cameras at Pier 54, he lead the assembly in presenting a loving cup to the *Carpathia*'s skipper and medals to his officers and crew.

Throughout the ordeal of meeting the press, Dorothy managed to keep up her sense of humor. When receiving columnist Chauncey Parsons, she apologized for her appearance. "These are not my clothes at all," she said, smiling. "I was fortunate enough to have a chum just my size who fitted me out as soon as I landed in New York. A white silk evening dress will do to escape in from a sinking liner, but it would look rather queer on the street in the afternoon." No explanation was necessary for Parsons who was charmed by Dorothy. He found her "pretty and cheerful" — in fact not at all "like a Robinson Crusoe, for her startling experiences on the *Titanic* have left few traces." Asked by Parsons about future vacations, Dorothy said she had had "quite enough of ocean travel for some time," adding that

Europe offers no inducements now that can drag me away from the Western shore of the Atlantic. The whole adventure was so unreal that it seems more like a story I have read. But I don't care to read any more like it.

Her interview in *Moving Picture News* was similarly entertaining, showing her high-spirited directness, such as when she told the writer that "it would take more than a shipwreck to knock her out." But Dorothy's composure was less convincing to that reporter than it had been to Parsons, the *News* article stating that she "has the appearance of one whose nerves had been greatly shocked." Her physical travail aside, Dorothy assured her fans she was resuming work at once.

Coming back to the studios at Fort Lee might normally have been a jubilant occasion for Dorothy but to return to act in a film about the disaster she had just survived was a disturbing prospect. How this ambitious proposition was initiated isn't clear; there are various versions. According to press releases from Éclair, Dorothy had resisted the proposition that she appear in a movie depicting the tragedy but had finally relented "in order to tell the true story." As the *Moving Picture World* put it:

> *It was a nerve-racking task but, like actresses before the footlights, this beautiful young cinematic star valiantly conquered her feelings and went through the work.*

In later years, Dorothy claimed it was more or less her idea, that her "instinct as an actress propelled me" as well as her desire to "share the truth of the sinking." Dorothy was proactive (when it suited her) and, since she wrote the scenario for the film, it's possible the final decision to commit the story to the screen was hers. However, the rumor that it was entirely Julie's brainchild might also be true. As an Éclair advisor and producer, and president of the firm that distributed Éclair's movies, it's not far-fetched that Brulatour recommended a script be eked out of the *Titanic* story for profit. After all, his own newsreel production company was one of the first to record the disaster. His personal interest in the company's leading lady, an open secret with its management, lends further weight to this version of the tale. If his later reputation as a taskmaster, almost a Svengali, can be believed, it's possible Julie may even have used his power to convince Dorothy to play her most famous role against her wishes.

Whatever the genesis of the picture, preparation for it began within two days of Dorothy's arrival home. While Éclair manager Harry Raver assumed the official role of producer (with Brulatour as silent partner) and arranged for construction to begin on the set at Fort Lee, director Etienne Arnaud, his camera crew and a group of extra actors accompanied Dorothy to New York Harbor. There a land-bound, derelict freighter had been hired to serve as the backdrop for the movie's shipboard scenes. Being near the dock where she had come ashore from her real-life nightmare voyage ensured the right atmosphere and incentive for Dorothy to portray genuine feeling. According to reporters who were on hand to record the unique incident, Dorothy was unnerved at the sight of the wrecked, listing boat. She was even more distressed by the frantic prompting of Arnaud and his cinematographers, which brought back the fear she had felt only a few days earlier. To add to the setting's surreal atmosphere, Dorothy was wearing the same dress, sweater, coat and hat she had worn the night of her escape in the lifeboat.

A correspondent for the *Harrisburg Leader* best described the reaction from the crew and extras as they watched one of the affecting scenes that resulted from this location shoot. In the scene Dorothy was to portray her realization that the *Titanic* was going down.

A LIVING MEMORY

As close-up shots were made of her standing by a rail, she drew on her well-known ability to register emotion through subtle gesture. In his story for the *Leader*, published April 21, the reporter observed:

> *As the cameramen advanced upon her alone on the deck of this supposedly doomed ship, they witnessed a tragic bit of acting that stirred even their hearts, accustomed as they were to weekly scenes of the kind.*

The article asserted that while Dorothy went through her solo scenes, the cast and crew, standing by, acknowledged that hers "was real acting," and congratulated themselves on being associated with such "a heroic little lady." Shooting continued, but eventually Dorothy "became overwhelmed." Arnaud ordered the cameras stopped and several supporting players ran to console her. Explained the *Leader*: "She had practically lost her reason by virtue of the terrible strain she had been under to graphically portray her part." Filming was suspended for the remainder of the day while the star was ordered to rest.

Dorothy's dedication to the project won praise from much of the motion picture press, although some publications questioned the taste and timing of such a sensitive subject. An editorial in the *Moving Picture World* recommended that the *Titanic* disaster be discouraged as an exhibition feature, while Dorothy and Éclair were excoriated in a May 8 column by The Spectator in the *Dramatic Mirror*.

> *The announcement by an independent company of good repute that it would produce a film based on the sea horror, and feature an actress fortunate enough to come out of the ship alive, can occasion only apprehension of the gravest character.*

Though the pseudonymous reviewer admitted the story might be "treated with good taste" and "not insult a mourning nation," he wrote that he expected the worst:

> *The flamboyant style of advertising announcing the proposed film does not give much hope that the subject will be treated in a seemly manner. It is feared the film will be a melodramatic affair that will inevitably fall absurdly short of truth and hence prove a lamentable travesty.*

In sharing his opinion of Dorothy Gibson, The Spectator went in for the kill:

> *The bare idea of undertaking to reproduce in a studio, no matter how well - equipped, an event of the appalling character of the* Titanic *disaster, with its 1,600 victims, is revolting, especially at this time when the horrors of the event are so fresh in mind. And that a young woman who came so lately, with her good mother, safely through the distressing scenes can now bring herself to commercialize her good fortune, is past understanding.*

The columnist's stance was motivated by the recent backlash from movie patrons toward

FINDING DOROTHY

theatres that had advertised and presented bogus *Titanic* newsreels, complete with altered images of other ships and even recreated scenes of the *Titanic*'s sinking and the rescue of her survivors. One such newsreel was allegedly stopped while in progress and the theatre closed by the police after a number of moviegoers had complained of being duped. In the wake of this rabblement, Brulatour set a high criterion for responsible newsreel reporting of the tragedy when the seventh edition of his *Animated Weekly* program was released to East Coast exhibitors on April 22.

A *Billboard* correspondent who was in the crowd that packed New York's Weber's Theatre three days later, wrote that reaction from audiences, which included several *Titanic* survivors at one showing, was highly emotional. *Billboard* congratulated the Sales Company for being "the first on the scene (in New York Harbor) with specially chartered tugboats and an extra relay of cameramen." The *Dramatic Mirror* also praised Brulatour's company for the "distinct care and order" it took in producing so expediently the compilation of scenes for the *Animated Weekly:*

> *That the motion picture may fairly equal the press in bringing out a timely subject and one of startling interest to the public at large was most efficiently demonstrated by the issuing of this film so soon after the event.*

Julie patted himself on the back by placing advertisements and news items about the "giant scoop" he had scored with his "*Titanic* Wreck" newsreel. Released as a "special exclusive," he billed it as "The Most Famous Film in the Whole World," which it seems to have been. The *Animated Weekly*'s *Titanic* edition attracted thousands of people and other newsreels paid to use footage from it. Weber's Theatre, in particular, was jammed with audiences day and night. Guglielmo Marconi, the famous inventor of wireless, was even given a private screening at Weber's when he attended with friends after hours, and in Washington. D.C., it was reported that senators recessed from Capitol Hill meetings to view it when it opened. Among the *Animated Weekly*'s stirring images, projected to a melancholy piano score and many a teary eye, were shots of the laying of *Titanic*'s keel and its launching. There were also scenes of icebergs in the region near where the *Titanic* sank, captured by a Sales Company photographer on a voyage a week before. Pictures of Captain Smith on the bridge of the *Olympic*, the *Titanic*'s sister ship, were also shown. Although there were no images to present of the *Titanic*'s destruction, the appropriate mood was conveyed through a dark title card, silence and the ghostly appearance on the screen of those three letters now familiar to all the world — "C.Q.D."

The *Dramtic Mirror* reporter's own feelings were evident in the piece, which he concluded by saying that the "amazing" *Animated Weekly* scenes he witnessed were "a remarkable achievement" and that they would "live in the memory as long as man exists." A number of shots from this issue of Brulatour's *Animated Weekly* survive in film archives today. It is to him, and to preservationists, that history owes a debt of gratitude. Few knew of Julie's peculiar connection to the *Titanic* story — that his mistress had nearly lost her life in the sinking — but there was no doubt in the public's mind as to the pride he took in the production of this special newsreel. On May 4, it was reported that Brulatour had communicated with President William Howard Taft to offer him a copy of the film. The Presi-

71

dent, in mourning for his friend and advisor, Major Archie Butt, who was lost in the sinking, graciously accepted, and the newsreel was duly deposited, at Taft's personal request, in the collection of the Library of Congress.

Eclair, aware that the delicate nature of their own *Titanic* picture could cause a furor like that which had attended less ethical productions, was anxious to avoid angering a public still shocked by the disaster. To this end, at Brulatour's insistence, the studio outlined its objectives in making the film and boomed Dorothy's involvement in the production, not only as its star, but also as the author of the story on which the script was based. A lengthy article in the *New York Daily Telegraph* of April 28 informed movie fans that Éclair's coming special feature was now officially entitled *Saved From the Titanic:*

> *The drama is written by Miss Gibson from her own experiences, which were, for the most part, too harrowing to be recorded. However, (she) has made a gripping naval story of love and tragedy, founded upon the sad catastrophe that in no wise will offend the sensibilities of the public, which still feels the terrible bitterness of the accident. ... Miss Gibson had a great deal of trouble during the posing and preparation of the picture; it was a harrowing piece of work to go over the details of the terrible experience. But the actress behind the footlights, the young cinematic star, stuck to her art for the sake of a good production.*

The announcement, which included plenty of motion picture industry hyperbole, also provided practical descriptions of the new movie's studio sets and special effects. According to the *Daily Telegraph,* work had been completed on:

> *a miniature vessel and a studio-built ocean and iceberg, effecting a clever reproduction of the terrible affair as visualized through a nightmare of memory by Miss Gibson .... The wireless room, the sinking of the great ship, a United States battleship, the rescue and the terrible effects are all features of the play, which will enthrall spectators the more so because they will know that the production was prepared and starred in by this brave young woman.*

The *Daily Telegraph* couldn't say enough about the star or her script, which "has the love element and heart interest necessary to carry an appeal." Readers had no way of knowing that the "love element" and "heart interest" of Dorothy's scenario were as authentic as the movie's depictions of the shipwreck. The basic plot of Dorothy's screenplay was that, as her alter ego "Miss Dorothy," she is returning home on board the *Titanic* to be engaged to a young military officer, "Ensign Jack." Anxious for word of his traveling sweetheart, Jack goes with a friend to see another pal who is a radio operator. While the three men prepare to send Dorothy a wireless, they hear the *Titanic*'s distress signal.

As a synopsis published in the *Moving Picture World* of May 11 read: "No pen can depict the anguish of the young man and the scene the next day when he calls upon Dorothy's father and mother." The portion of the film showing her experiences on the *Titanic* is revealed in the form of flashbacks as a rescue-thankful Dorothy sits at her parents' dining room table and relates the events. A staple silent film effect is achieved when Dorothy faints from the stress of telling her tale. This seems to be one of several overwrought plot tactics — another being a patriotic subtext, first suggested in the use of a Navy cruiser as a stand-in for the civilian rescue ship. The conclusion of *Saved From the Titanic* involves Dorothy's mother appealing to Jack, on behalf of her prostrate daughter, to give up his naval career. Here the father steps in and, refusing to hear of such a promise, tells Jack that a man's duty to his country is foremost. He sends for Dorothy and points her toward Jack with the line, "My daughter, there's your husband."

The final scenes are of the lovers embracing, intercut with a close up of a billowing flag and Dorothy's father looking on with pride. The scenario, though slight, was nonetheless intense, given the widespread appeal of the *Titanic* aspect. Privately for Dorothy, the film wasn't so much autobiographical as it was wish-fulfillment. At least on screen, she could see herself getting her man in the end. Her script also illuminated the characters of her real-life parents: God-fearing Leonard and meddlesome Pauline.

American audiences finally got their chance to see *Saved From the Titanic* on May 16, Éclair having missed its scheduled release date by two days, owing to last minute editing complications. Coming out as it did almost a month to the day of the actual sinking of *Titanic* (and the day before Dorothy's 23rd birthday), the Éclair film may have set a record for film production. "In 1912 there was generally a period of about two months for a one-reel film to be produced, processed and distributed to theatres," wrote movie historian Frank Thompson in his book, *Lost Films*. "*Saved From the Titanic* cut that schedule to less than half." Though touted as a special feature, the picture was the standard distribution length. At just over 300 meters, it was also (gauging by contemporary projection speed guidelines for movie houses) only about 12-15 minutes in duration.

For the public, the film was long enough to prove a winner. At the Lyric Theatre, favored home of Éclair films in New York City, the house was "packed for weeks," Dorothy recalled. With the star's inspired performance, a supporting cast culled from Éclair's finest stock players and Arnaud's artistic cinematography, the picture was a hit, easily surpassing the huge sales Éclair had enjoyed with its debut films, *Hands Across the Sea* and *Miss Masquerader*. Dorothy's costars — Jack Adolfi (as Jack), Alec Francis (as Father), Julia Stuart (as Mother) and Guy Oliver and William Dunn (as Jack's pals) — shared her pride in the movie's success. Also appearing on screen, as Dorothy's friends, were Muriel Ostriche and Isabel Lamon, which gave another realistic touch.

At last Dorothy could rest, knowing the film was being received well by fans all over the country. It would afford her an opportunity to plan the next fateful step in her life. She and Julie enjoyed the acclaim the film was winning and the profits it was making; they also must have had a good laugh at a caper Brulatour pulled. On the day *Saved From the Titanic* was released, a lesser Éclair vehicle was shown, probably as part of the same program. It was called *Roses and Thorns*, a fluffy society comedy financed by Julie. That wasn't so out of the ordinary, but the actor playing a chauffeur in the movie certainly was — Jules Brulatour himself. It was a lark, but also interesting symbolism. Julie was definitely behind the wheel of Éclair — and of Dorothy Gibson. *Roses and Thorns* indeed.

Meanwhile, *Saved From the Titanic* continued its strong hold on audiences. Movie houses across the nation, even in small towns, reported sell-out showings. Reviews in magazines like *Moving Picture News* give a glimpse of the reception accorded the film at its release:

> *The startling story of the sea's greatest sea disaster is the sensation of the country. Miss Dorothy Gibson, a heroine of the shipwreck and one of the most talked-of survivors, tells in this motion picture masterpiece of the enthralling tragedy among the icebergs.*

The *News* singled out the technical achievements of the "realistic" and "magnificently acted" movie, especially its "wonderful mechanical and lighting effects." It also made a point to state that the

> *harassing details that might offend good taste are carefully omitted, but the story of the wreck, the love interest, and the effects of the bitter calamity are all depicted.*

Even the *Moving Picture World,* which had earlier expressed concern about the *Titanic* being exploited in cinema, lauded the movie in its May 11 issue.

> *Miss Dorothy Gibson, one of the survivors of the great disaster .... has performed a unique piece of acting in the sensational new film-play of the Éclair Company .... It is the story of the wreck, founded upon Miss Gibson's own experiences, and with a lot of the mechanical and vision pictures which have made fame for Éclair's American directors, the film is creating a great activity in the market, for interest in the catastrophe has made a national demand. Miss Gibson had hardly recovered from her terrible strain in the wreck when she was called upon to take part in this new piece, which she constructed as well .... A surprising and artistically perfect reel has resulted.*

The film was shown in the U.S. throughout the spring and summer of 1912. The demand for *Saved From the Titanic* was so great that in cities where it had not yet been screened, exhibitors ran Dorothy's other movies, advertising in print ads and on posters that the star was a *Titanic* survivor. By this tactic, the manager of the Lyric Theatre in Mena, Arkansas drew hundreds of patrons in to see Dorothy's *The Wrong Bottle*. And in Amsterdam, New York, the Ideal Theatre announced to customers that in its presentation of *The Legend of Sleepy Hollow* "will be seen Miss Dorothy Gibson, one of the survivors of the *Titanic* disaster."

On July 25 *Saved From the Titanic* was released in Great Britain, under the title, *A Survivor of the Titanic,* a more direct representation of the movie's content, though less artistic. (The original title is believed to have been taken from an April 24 headline in the *Dramatic Mirror,* announcing Dorothy's escape from the ship) The movie showed to full

FINDING DOROTHY

theatres in England and in other countries as well, including France, where it was ecstatically reviewed by *Cine-Journal* on its release there in June. Despite its popularity, this gem of cinematic history is lost to modern audiences. As earlier mentioned, not many of Éclair's American films have been preserved. To have so few examples of the output of this important early studio is in itself a loss to the history of motion pictures. But that Éclair's first film (*Hands Across the Sea*) and one of its most celebrated (*Saved From the Titanic*) are among the titles no longer in existence makes the loss all the worse to cinema historians.

To scholars working in the field of ocean liner research, particularly those making *Titanic* a focus, the loss of this nugget of history is also felt. The hope is great among historians in both fields that *Saved From the Titanic* will one day be retrieved from some obscure collection, tucked away in a forgotten vault or attic. "No matter what melodramatic hokum found its way into the film — and the synopsis suggests that there was plenty — *Saved From the Titanic* is an irreplaceable piece of *Titanic* lore," commented Frank Thompson. It's exciting enough that even one of Dorothy Gibson's lost films has been found. When *The Lucky Holdup* is made available commercially, it will be a treat for the film aficionado to assess the appeal and capabilities of one of America's first bona fide movie stars. But to see her on screen as she reenacted her own experiences in history's most legendary sea disaster would be a coup. For the time being, film fans and nautical buffs have only the stills, advertisements and reviews of *Saved From the Titanic* by which to remember it. The camera panning in on Dorothy's stricken face as she replayed the fears that gripped her on the real *Titanic* can only be imagined.

Chapter 7:
Ready and Waiting
1912

BY THE SUMMER OF 1912, emoting was the last thing on Dorothy Gibson's mind. She had had enough of sorrow and wanted free of the memory of *Titanic* — and of the exigency of making films. Since her return home after the worst end to a vacation imaginable, she had thought of nothing but the disaster from which she was spared, and it had taken its toll on her. She was mentally and physically exhausted from the event and the subsequent re-staging of it for Éclair. As she began filling her time with Julie, she was again contented and focused. Yet her desire to leave motion pictures, which Harry Raver, Pat Casey, and Julie had dismissed as a mere need for a "good holiday," was stronger than ever. Her heart wasn't in the work, and she wanted out.

When later mentioning her decision to retire from acting, Dorothy gave no reason, except that she was "dissatisfied." She was pleased with the success she had made of herself, and enjoyed the relative novelty of being a star in the burgeoning picture industry. But she lacked professional ambition. "I winged my way into every job," she would recall. "I enjoyed the work, but my dream was to marry and settle into a countrified life with children and animals. I was really just an old-fashioned girl."

Back with Julie, Dorothy was convinced her dream could come true once he made good his oft-repeated promise to divorce Clara and marry her. There was the question of Dorothy's own marriage, which doesn't seem to have been dissolved yet either; friend Muriel Ostriche claimed Dorothy did not divorce Battier until 1917, although Brulatour's legal records cite the date as 1913. Dorothy never seems to have questioned either the morality or the viability of her position as Brulatour's mistress. In spite of her outward sharpness and confidence, her view of the world was as naïve as her approach to love. Blinded by Julie's wealth and power, she had compromised her values, placing her trust in a man who was fundamentally unfaithful. While deluding herself that happiness lay around the corner, she became an accomplice to his deceit and her own destruction.

Dorothy did not resign from Éclair until later in the year, but she didn't star in any films after mid-May. In its August 7 issue, the *Dramatic Mirror* assured fans that Dorothy was still with Éclair but was "taking a rest at present." Yet she never made another movie. Intriguingly, Dorothy said *Saved From the Titanic* was not her last film, but the next to last. This was technically true since *The Revenge of the Silk Masks*, the serial episode she had completed just before sailing for Europe in March, had been delayed in wide release by

FINDING DOROTHY

Saved From the Titanic. However, if Dorothy was referring to another film, research has yet to identify it. She did make a cameo, as did Julie, in the farce *Roses and Thorns,* released on the same day as *Saved From the Titanic.* According to the *Morning Telegraph* "all Éclair's beauties appear in this little comedy, forming a chorus in a procession of white roses." Brulatour's appearance in the film as a chauffeur, the *Moving Picture World* noted, was a role he relished in order to show off "one of his fine motor cars" and demonstrate his "great skill at the wheel."

The end of Dorothy's career in movies was affected without fanfare. Éclair issued no press release, and Dorothy gave no interviews. She simply left her dressing room at Fort Lee one day and never returned. Although she had been in the film business for just over a year and had spent only 10 months as a leading lady with Éclair, Dorothy had enjoyed what many actresses never achieve in a lifetime. She had become a star. Along the way she had perfected a technique and personality that marked her as a solidly good actress. Yet her popularity on the screen meant little, if anything, to her. She was in love and wanted to be married. That was her ambition, and it would be her downfall.

Julie's obsession with Dorothy was already jeopardizing her career and would soon ravage her reputation. For Dorothy's part, she was a willing participant in an affair that would not only prevent her from attaining her full potential as an actress but lead her deeper into a relationship that was to result in a scandal that would dash any hopes of future professional success. But it was several years before she realized the misstep she had made in leaving her work to become Brulatour's plaything.

With Dorothy attending to her new life, which included sitting briefly for Harrison Fisher again, Éclair pressed on without her. She was replaced as leading lady by a young English dancer named Barbara Tennant. The newcomer was selected for her large expressive eyes, which were judged similar to Dorothy's by Eclair management. Her full face also reminded fans of Dorothy, although Tennant tended to appear stout and, in some pictures, rather double-chinned. Despite her faults, the string of Arnaud-directed films for which Dorothy had been called back from Italy to star in, were immediately reassigned to Tennant. The first of these was released May 21. Tennant's film presence struck a chord with fans and quickly established her as a major asset for Éclair. She would prove this later that summer in her role as Maid Marian in Arnaud's *Robin Hood*, the biggest project for the studio since *Saved From the Titanic.* It was the first time the familiar story was shown to American movie audiences and a great deal of publicity occasioned its release. Ironically, this movie, in which the character of Marian would have been played by Dorothy had she remained with Éclair, is one of the company's few surviving films from this date. Recently rescued and restored by the Fort Lee Film Commission, it features all of Dorothy's old costars — Jack Adolfi, Alec Francis, Julia Stuart, Muriel Ostriche. If Dorothy had stuck it out, silent fans would have been able to see her in this classic tale.

As Dorothy Gibson's star waned, Barbara Tennant's rose, thanks to a heady publicity campaign which erroneously claimed *she* was a *Titanic* survivor. Yet Dorothy remained a part of the thriving East Coast movie community, maintaining her friendships with erstwhile Fort Lee costars like Pearl White, Lamar Johnstone and Muriel Ostriche. That fans missed Dorothy was indicated by their letters asking about her well into 1913; some of these were printed in the *Morning Telegraph, Dramatic Mirror* and the *Moving Picture World*. The former "Harrison Fisher Girl" attended all the motion picture balls and, as some of her films continued to be shown across the country, she was still a recognizable face as late as 1915 when, at the Brighton Beach Film Carnival, she joined a parade of stars that included Clara Kimball Young, Fannie Ward, Francis X. Bushman and Maurice Costello.

Dorothy heard all about the latest movie doings through Julie, who was becoming daily more important in the rapidly growing motion picture industry. Just before Dorothy quit the movies, a huge step in the history of the medium was taken with the formation of the Universal Film Manufacturing Company, later known as Universal Pictures. Brulatour was a driving force in establishing the new corporation, having been approached in February by fellow luminary Laemmle, Dorothy's old employer, to assist him in drawing together the support of competing studios in what would prove an unprecedented amalgamation of talent and resources. Still chief of the Sales Company, the valiant supply, distribution and lobbying arm of the independent filmmakers, Julie was arguably the most powerful man in the movie business in 1912. His prolific financing of the Fort Lee compound as well as its newest and most promising studio, Éclair, made Julie the ideal partner for Laemmle in his plans to pummel once and for all Edison's Motion Picture Patents Company. Offering his agency not only as the sole distributor of Eastman film stock but as the financial representative of Éclair, whose Fort Lee plant Laemmle wanted to buy, Brulatour came on board as a full partner in the enterprise.

By unanimous resolution at a meeting held in Julie's office on May 13, some fourteen companies, including Éclair as the most desirable of the group, were successfully merged to constitute Universal. It was a complicated deal, accomplished through Laemmle's passion and Brulatour's diplomacy. The new confederation with its message of solidarity against the monopoly of Edison's "Sacred Eight" was announced in the press on May 18 and formally incorporated on June 5. News reports stressed that the new association was "much strengthened by the addition of the Éclair films."

Despite Brulatour's high hopes for Universal, which he served as the new concern's first president, his involvement was brief and turbulent. When George Eastman learned that he was offering the Universal producers a significantly reduced rate on stock, he notified Julie of his objections, asserting that the new partnership was a conflict of interest, and threatened to cut off his film supply if he didn't withdraw his agency from Universal. At the end of June, Brulatour, who had already relinquished his presidency to Charles O. Baumann, presented Eastman's demands at an emergency session of the Universal board of directors and asked to be allowed to resign, "fearing illegality," as *Billboard* noted. The committee, except for Baumann, who was not in town, reluctantly approved his withdrawal from the board. Anticipating the storm that was brewing, Julie left for France for a secret summer holiday with Dorothy. They sailed from New York aboard *La Provence* on June 20 for what Brulatour admitted to reporters was a "pleasure trip." For Dorothy, being whisked away (apparently incognito) by her lover on this spontaneous vacation, was the tonic she

FINDING DOROTHY

needed.

That their romance had become carefully orchestrated by this time is obvious, since Jules' wife and children were also in Europe on holiday. But having to share Julie was something Dorothy had grown accustomed to, even on vacation, and it didn't interfere with her hopes of the alter. What's more, as had happened at the time of courting George Battier, Harrison Fisher's magical way with the brush again touched her life, creating a fantasy vignette that not only used her image but seemed to capture her innermost longings. Maybe Fisher had been inspired by the ending of *Saved From the Titanic* when, for the June 1912 issue of the *Ladies Home Journal*, he chose Dorothy as the model for his depiction of a bride having last-minute touches applied to her wedding dress. This imaginary scene must have pleased Dorothy; she may even have carried a copy of the magazine on her Parisian getaway to flesh out her daydreams.

Brulatour had no time for fantasies. When the pair returned home a month later, most of the dreaded damage to his association with Universal had been done. Harry Raver, who had served as secretary of the Supply Company, the Sales Company's off-shoot, had followed Brulatour's example and resigned from his position as Éclair manager to prevent any further accusations of conflict of interest. Meantime, Éclair CEO Charles Jourjon had pulled out of negotiations with an incensed Laemmle for the sale of his Fort Lee studio. Ultimately, Baumann stepped down as president of Universal, following a quarrel with Laemmle over Julie's resignation, Baumann claiming the board had no right to allow Brulatour to withdraw without his consent. But Julie wasn't out of the fray yet. On top of all else, a virtual war broke out between Brulatour and his former partner Raver, now general manager of the Supply Company, for the right to distribute Eclair's films. As the Supply Company and Éclair were controlled by Universal, Laemmle reserved the right to choose Raver as his distributor over Julie. But Brulatour had been wise enough during his trip to Paris to get the owners of Éclair to sign a contract, designating him as sole distributor, thereby reverting to their original agreement before the advent of Universal.

Fearing the loss to his new organization if Éclair removed itself from the fold completely, Laemmle went to work unruffling feathers on both sides of the Atlantic, with the result that Éclair remained with Universal. How Brulatour was appeased in this deal, a definite loss to his Sales Company, is not known. Despite its eventual unhappy outcome for Julie personally, the consolidation of the leading independent filmmakers under the umbrella of Universal was a major turning point in the history of American filmmaking. The merger not only signaled the triumph of a free market in motion pictures but lead to the creation of the first major Hollywood studio — Universal City, constructed in 1914-15 in Los Angeles in an effort by Laemmle to centralize operations. The part Brulatour played in the historic amalgam can't be underestimated. Nor can the influence of Éclair. Nor in turn, the success of its first leading lady, the now retired Dorothy Gibson, whose comedies (and one titanic drama in particular) helped crystallize the studio's reputation for quality and originality.

Chapter 8:
My Lady Drives
1912-1913

AFTER HER RESIGNATION FROM ECLAIR, Dorothy centered her life around Julie. Maybe she hoped her brush with death might spur her lover down the aisle. But she had a long wait ahead of her. In this instance, life would not imitate art; Jules Brulatour was no Ensign Jack. Almost nothing is known of the pair's domestic existence, if there was one at this time. It appears Dorothy continued to live in her apartment on West 148th Street while the Brulatours resided on West End Avenue. From what can be determined, Pauline shared the flat with her daughter. Meantime, her father maintained the family home in Manhattan.

With no central meeting place, Dorothy still saw Julie several evenings a week in New York City hotels. The couple also spent occasional weekends away, and when Brulatour took business trips to Philadelphia and Chicago, which he did frequently to meet with new clients or with representatives of his exchange offices, Dorothy sometimes accompanied him. When Julie's wife traveled with their children to visit relatives in the west, he seized the opportunity to go out with Dorothy to plays, the opera and nightclubs. Her nights were reserved for Julie but by day Mutsie was busy singing for her supper — or hoping to. Bored without the modeling and acting work that had taken up so much of her time, Dorothy decided to enroll in singing courses to refine her voice in hopes of pursuing an operatic career. Through classes taught by coaches affiliated with the Metropolitan Opera House, Dorothy was learning to apply herself to music beyond the popular tunes with which she entertained friends. Dorothy loved singing as much as ever, and her exposure to grand opera through Julie had inspired her to seek vocal education from some of New York's top instructors.

"The great Gatti-Cassazza of the Metropolitan heard me sing at a reception," Dorothy bragged. "He said I had an uncommon voice that should be improved upon and persuaded me to study." Brulatour supported her in her newest endeavor but that she was serious about becoming a great soprano, or even thought she had the required talent, seems unlikely. It was a way to amuse Julie, whose passion for the operatic stage she wanted to share. It was belting out Irving Berlin rags that came naturally to Dorothy. So from club to theatre to opera to cocktail party, interspersed with luncheons and dinners (and lovemaking in suites all over town), Julie and Mutsie, like masked guests at a rococo ball, went on playing their dangerous game of romance. But these modern revelers' escapades were eventually

FINDING DOROTHY

discovered. How Clara Brulatour learned of their affair isn't known. Perhaps she heard that Julie hadn't been alone on his summer trip to Paris or that he was in the habit of paying for another woman's clothes, couturiers being notorious for sending a mistress' dress bills to the wife "by mistake." It may have been a simple case of his being seen out with Dorothy by Clara's friends. A man of his distinction wouldn't go unnoticed in public, especially when escorting a woman who was not his wife. Society's wagging tongues did their bit.

It could not have eased Clara's mind to know that the "other woman" was the pretty young actress whose films Brulatour had been backing for over a year. How his wife confronted Julie about his affair, or when, is not recorded, but it happened before the end of 1912. What is certain is that Clara wanted a divorce, and she started proceedings against her husband immediately. Julie also wanted free but feared the publicity of a court battle. Clara reconsidered and withdrew the suit, the Brulatours finally agreeing on a compromise in the form of a separation contract that would not involve the courts. Under the terms of this bargain, Clara would receive an annuity of $20,000 for herself and the couple's three children. Although her lawyers attempted to extract a larger allotment from Julie, Clara ultimately accepted his offer, stipulating that he insure his life for $65,000 to her benefit. Julie consented, and he and Clara signed the pact. As Clara underwent the agony of the dissolution of her marriage, all seemed to be going well for Dorothy and her dreams of matrimony — but only for the time being.

The year 1913 dawned on big hopes and plans for Dorothy. She now had use of the Brulatours' former summer house and gardens on Long Island Sound, where she stayed on weekends. It was finally coming together for her. Wedding or no wedding, Mutsie might at least have her countrified life. A business matter involving the memory of the *Titanic* encroached briefly on Dorothy's idyllic winter world when she and her mother filed formal claims against the White Star Line for the loss of their property in the sinking. The official petitioner, Oceanic Steam Navigation Company, a J.P. Morgan conglomerate which was the ultimate owner of *Titanic*, was bombarded with claims from passengers and crew in the wake of the disaster. Dorothy signed her damage suit in district court on January 31, following her mother's claim by a week. Through their attorneys, Hunt, Hill and Betts, the women asked to be compensated in the combined amount of $3,866.50, a modest sum compared to other petitions from first class passengers.

The itemized listing of the Gibsons' possessions included everything from a thimble and scissors (in Pauline's luggage) to a barette and two hairpins (in Dorothy's); the ladies missed nothing in their accounting. The most expensive single article in either inventory was Dorothy's $300 fur muff. The most curious item was a $150 diamond crescent brooch, which both women claimed. Like most survivors, Dorothy and Pauline would receive only a fraction of the money they asked for. It's interesting that the women filed their *Titanic* claims just before they boarded another ship for what would be their first sailing together since the tragedy. On February 8, accompanied by Julie, the Gibsons set off from New York on the North German-Lloyd Liner *Victoria Luise*. En route to Wiesbaden via

MY LADY DRIVES

Paris, the vacation was a thrill for Dorothy, as much for Julie's company as for the spas. Wiesbaden was full of Americans that winter, and the three no doubt found many friends in the crowd. Mother and daughter might even have encountered some of their fellow *Titanic* survivors at the resort. In fact, Molly Brown, the indomitable heroine of the disaster, Lady Duff Gordon, famous as the dress designer "Lucile," and fashion columnist Edith Rosenbaum were all in Weisbaden at that time. Pauline, Dorothy and Julie spent nearly a month in Germany. They returned to New York, again aboard the *Victoria Luise*, on March 8. What happened on their return would forever change their lives.

While heading out of New York City to the bungalow on Long Island, merrily at the wheel of the little gray car Julie had given her, Dorothy was distracted by a passing motorist. Although she had averted her view of the road for what she would claim was "but an instant," it was sufficient for her to lose control of the car and veer onto a walkway, striking two pedestrians, a married couple. The car, a 1912 Detroit Electric, rolled completely over them, killing the man and seriously injuring the lady. This tragedy not only took a life and threatened another, but began a series of virulent public blows to Dorothy's reputation. The woman hurt in the accident, Julia Smith, promptly sued Jules Brulatour for $25,000 for the loss of her husband and her own injuries. Julie's lawyers were successful in keeping the case from the press for a while, but by the end of May the news of the sensational circumstances — a young woman "running down a man" while driving her married lover's car — was revealed at the trial. That the young woman was none other than the "Harrison Fisher Girl" and a once-popular movie actress, and her paramour a millionaire film tycoon, provided all the necessary spice for a tabloid scandal. As the media lapped up the revelations, Dorothy, Brulatour and their families, were devastated.

Crucial testimony from Dorothy sealed her fate. Cross-examined in court before Justice Platzek, Smith's attorneys went for the jugular. Asked about her relationship with the owner of the vehicle, Dorothy, tense and pale-faced in the witness box, was forced to reveal that they were "good friends" and had "visited each another." Asked how long she had had use of the car, she answered that she had driven it "for over a year." Finally, as the *New York Times* reported, Dorothy was asked "if she was acquainted with *Mrs.* Brulatour." The proverbial pin-drop reverberated throughout the courtroom when she replied, simply, "No." The drama continued when Julie, shortly after taking the stand, objected angrily to questions about his marital woes. "I am a gentleman!" he shouted.

At the trial's resumption on May 21, following a brief break, Judge Platzek announced that the litigants had reached an agreement. He then directed the jury to award Smith $4,500. Why the woman consented to such a drastic reduction isn't known but it may be that, since the trial had become more notable for the destructive gossip it was generating, Smith had been convinced to settle in order to rid herself of the scrutiny of the press. If Smith's discounted windfall was an anticlimax to the lawsuit, Julie made up for it with an ill-timed attempt to defend Dorothy. According to the *New York Times:*

> Brulatour volunteered the information that although he was not divorced from his wife, Dorothy Gibson was his fiancee and that he intended marrying her as soon as his wife obtained her divorce. In making this statement, Brulatour addressed himself directly to Justice Platzek, explaining that he wanted to counteract any in-

sinuations which might be made at the trial.

Since the Brulatours' divorce had actually been withdrawn by Clara, who had agreed to a separation deal instead, Julie's statement in court came as a shock to her. When the couple had separated the previous year, only Julie's commitment to insure himself per their contract remained to be carried out. He had resisted taking out the insurance, however, and the case brought by Smith had further delayed his fulfilling that obligation. Humiliated and incensed by her husband's remarks, which were quoted in newspapers all over the country, Clara Brulatour reopened her divorce suit.

Chapter 9:
Love Finds a Way
1913-1916

REELING FROM HER OWN PUBLIC EMBARRASSMENT, Dorothy immersed herself in the country. Her operatic lessons continued, conducted by a succession of teachers who now came out to Long Island. She also practiced with the promising young German tenor Johannes Sembach, with whom she may have had an affair. Perhaps she found in the music that emanated from her little cottage the strength she needed to face the brutal facts of the life she had chosen. She definitely found a bit of amusement at this time in picking up copies of Harrison Fisher's latest series of albums — *Beauties* and *The Little Gift Book*. Both volumes contained several illustrations of Dorothy, among which were such favorites as "Roses," "Bows Attract Beaus," and "Well Protected." The latter, chosen for the cover of the *Ladies Home Journal* that February, was one of Fisher's last portraits of Dorothy, painted just over a year earlier. Actually a composite picture, melding Dorothy's features with those of Fisher's earlier muse, Rita Rasmussen, it would become better known by its postcard incarnation, copies of which sold in the millions. Showing a fur-coated, puppy-hugging Dorothy/Rita in a big green hat, the portrait remains one of Fisher's most representative and collectible images from this period.

"Well Protected" was one of the last Dorothy Gibson-inspired illustrations by Harrison Fisher to appear as magazine cover art. For the record, rival model Margery Allwork claimed it was she alone who posed for this picture. Did Fisher use all three women as his inspiration? Perhaps, but it should be noted that Allwork, while admittedly the most prolific of Fisher's models, claimed to have posed for several pictures that Mary Elizabeth Forbes is known definitely to have sat for. The Harrison Fisher books, with many of their plates depicting his new models, Alice Joyce, leading lady for Kalem Pictures, and Olive Thomas, the future Ziegfeld showgirl, were peeks into a different time for Dorothy. Then on the threshold of a budding career, she now stood on the precipice of defeat. A welcome respite from the media and courts came with a trip to Europe that summer. Traveling with Pauline as usual, she again took in the sights of Italy, France and England. The pair returned home in late August aboard the *Olympic*, the *Titanic*'s nearly identical sister ship. Though she felt her personal reputation was shattered, Dorothy consoled herself that she still had Julie's love, and she lost herself in it more than ever.

While his private world swung out of control, Brulatour's professional life couldn't have been more flourishing. By 1914, he was nearing the top of his game as the leading distributor of American motion pictures. Meantime, he remained the sole agent for imported Eastman film stock. Added to the fortune he was making out of these enterprises was his lucrative role as president of newly formed Paragon Pictures. But his continued involvement as financial backer to the string of studios utilizing the Fort Lee locale was perhaps the most visible component to his fame in the movie business at this time.

Approached by Charles Jourjon of the Éclair Company, now operating smoothly under the aegis of Universal, Julie agreed to subsidize the construction of larger studios for Peerless Pictures in 1914, which added significantly to the technological and artistic capabilities for filmmaking available at Fort Lee. At the same time he entered into a partnership with Lewis J. Selznick and William Brady to establish World Pictures, another Fort Lee-based studio. Brulatour also funded the rebuilding of Éclair's processing lab, storage vault and offices which caught fire on March 19, destroying original negatives for almost all of the company's films produced over the last three years. Cameraman Francois Doublier braved the intense heat and smoke in an attempt to save some of the negatives but was overcome. Although hospitalized, he recovered. But several hundred negatives, apparently including those for all of Dorothy's movies, were lost.

Valued at over $200,000, the pictures represented more than monetary injury to Éclair — for historians, the lost Éclair *oeuvre* is an irreplaceable gauge for charting the growth of this influential French-American chapter in filmmaking. The Éclair studio wasn't the only thing ablaze in Julie's life. Clara, who had sued him for divorce a second time, had again relented, favoring the earlier arranged settlement. She was still fighting mad, insisting he insure himself at once in her favor so that in the event of his death, she and their children would be protected. Once more Julie promised he would do so then, true to form, he demurred. He was still hesitating nearly a year later when Clara finally challenged him in court again, this time in the New York Supreme Court, hoping to force him to honor his contractual duty. On April 22, 1915, Clara Brulatour's application came before Justice Glegerich who, according to the *New York Times,* "reserved decision." The case was thereafter privately heard and settled, Julie at last being compelled to take out insurance in the sum of $65,000 with his wife as beneficiary. For the time being, the warring Brulatours took a breather.

As Julie tried to forget his marital troubles, he was happy his girlfriend's expensive vocal coaching was proving such a fine investment. Dorothy was hoping for a second chance at professional success when she accepted an offer from Giulio Gatti-Casazza to appear in the chorus of the world premiere of Umberto Giardano's *Madame Sans-Gene.* The opera would be an unqualified hit, dominating the Metropolitan Opera House's 1914-1915 season. Opening January 25, *Madame Sans-Gene*, based on Victorien Sardou's famous play, starred Geraldine Farrar, Giovanni Martinelli and Pasquale Amato. With a libretto by Renato Simoni, the production's music by Giardano (best known for *Fedora*), was much praised, particularly the orchestral score. Despite what were considered weak arias and an unsatisfactory

LOVE FINDS A WAY

third act, critics were largely impressed. According to a review in *Theatre Magazine* for March 1915:

> *The orchestra played superbly, the chorus sang wonderfully. Scenery and costumes were among the most effective shown on this great stage .... To sum up,* Madame Sans-Gene *is a clever, if not an inspired, opera, based on a fascinatingly interesting libretto, and faultlessly produced at the Metropolitan. It is again an offering to which Gatti-Casazza can point with pride.*

Vogue magazine for April 1, 1915 enthused about the production, especially the stage settings which "accomplished wonders" with their "brilliancy and effectiveness." Moreover, the reviewer found that "the excellence of the chorus contributed all that could be added to make the new opera a success." Dorothy took pride in appearing for the first time on the Metropolitan stage with none other than Geraldine Farrar. She reveled in press reviews congratulating the chorus, although she was never singled out by name.

She was worthy enough to be asked back by Gatti-Casazza, who put her into a series of productions thereafter. Dorothy, when recalling her operatic work, didn't cite specific shows, excepting *Madame Sans-Gene.* She did mention that she supported soprano Frieda Hempel in an unidentified production, presumably in 1915 or 1916. Cast lists for Metropolitan Opera House productions during these years do not include Dorothy Gibson. It's true that chorus members were not always credited in programmes but since many were in fact listed, the absence of her name is curious. It's likely therefore that, owing to the personal scandal she was still weathering, she opted to perform under an alias, as she had done when she began performing professionally. Credited or not, Dorothy never rose above the chorus to become a principal in any major operatic production, either at the Metropolitan or in Chicago, where she claimed to have appeared as well, possibly in a run of *La Tosca.* Her debut in such an important production as *Madame Sans-Gene,* even if only as a chorine, suggests she was a promising talent. The reason she didn't excel further may be that, as with modeling and film acting, she quickly tired of the work. Another possibility is that her shabby reputation, surely a liability in those days (at least when publicly exposed), prevented her being promoted to lead roles. When she wasn't performing, Dorothy was modeling again, this time for fashion photographer Ira Hill and several custom dressmaking salons, including Mme. Samuel and Plymouth Furs.

She was also still a regular at cocktail parties and other events in the movie community in New York and at Fort Lee. A social gathering of industry bigwigs at the World Film Company early in 1915 included Dorothy, and she joined the group for an impromptu photo afterward. Among the distinguished artists assembled were directors Albert Capellini, Emile Chautard, Maurice Tourneur and James Young, actors Frank Crane, Holbrook Blinn and Wilton Lackaye, and actresses Alice Brady, Elaine Hammerstein and Clara Kimball Young. Something of Dorothy's flirty personality is captured in the photo. Arm-in-arm with Lackaye, she averts her glance from the camera, instead aiming her charming smile in the direction of her flattered companion.

Although the caption for the image that appeared in the May 15, 1915 issue of *Moving Picture World* hinted that Dorothy was among World Film's new acquisitions,

FINDING DOROTHY

there's no evidence that she ever worked for the studio. It is interesting that the magazine considered her on a par with the others in the snapshot who were regarded as "without equal in respect to ability and money-earning power." In Dorothy's case, the claim probably referenced the huge popularity of *Saved From the Titanic,* which may still have been playing in theatres as a second billing feature in 1915.

Dorothy's new life corresponded with a spate of frenzied activity for Julie, who by early 1916 was working harder than ever to improve the appeal of Fort Lee for filmmakers, many of whom were now contemplating the move west to Hollywood, following the lead of Universal. In addition, Brulatour was named to the executive committee of the Motion Picture Board of Trade while George Eastman promoted him to head the entirety of the Eastman Kodak Company. Coincident with this appointment, Brulatour funded the construction of new studios for the Paragon Film Company at Fort Lee, including a facility specifically for the on-site production of Eastman stock. This structure, known as the Brulatour Building, still stands on Jane Street in the center of the old film colony.

Professionally, Fort Lee almost reentered Dorothy's life around this time when her friend Muriel Ostriche asked her to fill in for an actress who had fallen sick half-way through shooting a society farce for Equitable Pictures. Screenwriter Frances Marion also recommended Dorothy to director Charles Seay, who was agreeable to her stepping into the supporting role of a temperamental young matron in the film, *A Circus Romance.* The character would have been an ideal comeback for Dorothy, a perfect opportunity to reprise her comedic personality for screen fans. But Dorothy declined the offer. *A Circus Romance* was released February 5, 1916, while Dorothy was vacationing in Havana with her mother. By now Mutsie had given up her island cottage and garden for the spiffy, uptown trappings of a penthouse on Riverside Drive, a present from Julie. Mamma moved in and helped redecorate the luxury townhouse. If a tawdry item in the gossip magazine *Town Topics* has any merit, the centerpiece of the house was a huge mantel portrait after Drouais. Depicting a seductively posed Madame du Barry, Louis XV's luckless mistress, the painting's connotation was more apropos than Dorothy could have imagined.

Chapter 10:
The Awakening
1916-1924

BY 1916 JULES BRULATOUR was a very rich man. Apart from the fortune he had made while at Lumiere, which reportedly made him a millionaire, a conservative estimate of his earnings as chief of Eastman Kodak, as head of the Sales Company, and as an investor in Eclair and other companies, is considered to have been nearly $300,000. Julie's rising fame and influence soon spelled political power. When friend and partner William Brady was elected president of the National Association of the Motion Picture Industry (NAMPI) in 1917, he asked Julie to serve on the executive committee, alongside director D.W. Griffith and producer Adolf Zukor. With a membership comprised of representatives from all sectors of the business, the organization's objective was to function as a centralized public relations liaison between moviegoers and the film industry. When America entered the First World War, the group developed a special commission to assist the Federal Government in implementing public policy and initiatives through educational films and newsreels. As movie historian Leslie Midkiff de Bauche writes in her study *Reel Patriotism*, NAMPI's cooperation with the government

> *gave its members — the film companies, their leaders, their stars and theatre own-*
> *ers — the opportunity to integrate more fully with the many other industries mo-*
> *bilizing the homefront.*

Brulatour's involvement in NAMPI's War Cooperation Committee was pivotal. With his colleagues, Julie networked with the Treasury Department, the Food and Drug Administration, and other state and federal offices in distributing and promoting public welfare films to aid the government's Liberty Loan bond-selling tours, economy and conservation drives, heath programs and affiliated relief services like the American Red Cross. There is little doubt that Julie's sudden high profile in Washington determined him to legitimize his relationship with Dorothy Gibson; he may even have been pressured to do so. By now divorced from George Battier, Dorothy was ready to leap into the only role she ever wanted to play — that of Mrs. Jules Brulatour. One wonders why the pair had waited so long to tie the knot, both being free to do so by this stage. The problem seems to have been Julie's fear of Clara's litigious wrath, which would prove justified.

FINDING DOROTHY

The week before Brulatour was to join the War Cooperation Committee on Capitol Hill to confer with President Woodrow Wilson and his Council of National Defense, he was granted a divorce "on incompatible grounds" in the notoriously expedient Kentucky courts. On July 6, 1917 he finally married Dorothy in New York and the pair moved into a luxury apartment at 1067 Fifth Avenue. There, according to the *New York Clipper,* Julie "bestowed a considerable fortune" in jewels, clothes and furniture on his new bride. The couple spent their honeymoon in Washington, where on July 11 Julie and other NAMPI department officers met with the President, Treasury Secretary McAdoo and War Department Secretary Baker for the first of a series of conferences on how the motion picture industry could aid public understanding of wartime measures. The delegation of movie dignitaries was well received. As the *Exhibtors' Trade Review* reported:

> *The secretaries and heads of departments outdid one another in their enthusiasm over the power, influence and patriotism of the motion picture screen.*

The Brulatours continued their honeymoon in Chicago the following week where Julie and fellow officers presented a report of their Washington trip to the joint convention of the National Association of the Motion Picture Industry and the National Exhibitors Association. NAMPI would continue its collaboration with the Federal Government for the duration of the war, receiving high praise from the Wilson Administration and the public. The film division of Wilson's Committee of Public Information, of which journalist George Creel was appointed chairman, achieved considerably less success. Bringing along friends like Julie and Brady to sit on the executive board of this subcommittee, Creel endeavored to oversee censorship problems and propaganda methods. But arguments and financial troubles erupted from the beginning. Criticisms were also leveled at the men, among which were allegations of undue influence from media baron William Randolph Hearst, another of Creel's friends, and of kickbacks provided by Brulatour.

Despite this setback, Julie's wealth and political sway within the industry remained sound; his honesty and morality were secondary matters. The real impediment Julie encountered at this time was private. Clara, angered by his surprise marriage, filed a suit to annul the action, maintaining it was invalid as Julie wasn't a resident of Kentucky. Although she had twice pushed for divorce instead of separation, she now refused to accept the divorce Brulatour had obtained. Dorothy's response can only be imagined but there's no evidence that Julie attempted to set the matter straight and file for a New York divorce. Clara Brulatour wasn't going away, that was clear. The strife Dorothy had caused Julie's first wife was now her own, and the happiness she had longed for with him would never be. Strangely, Brulatour appears to have done nothing to rectify matters, reverting to his habit of empty promises. Of this trying period, Dorothy had little to say. "The marriage unfortunately was not a success," was her only comment. She gave no details of their brief and stormy married life. "Troubled from the start," as Dorothy's biographer Phillip Gowan put it, the union was really over before it began. Mutsie and Julie were no more.

Ironically, over the next two years, the Brulatours appeared a loving couple. They attended the premier of Griffith's war drama, *Hearts of the World*, and the opening of the third Liberty Loan drive on the Capitol steps. They also showed up together at the races and at various fund-raisers such as plays and concerts sponsored by the Stage Women's War Relief Society, of which Dorothy was a member. The Brulatours probably also attended productions benefiting the American Red Cross Association, of which they were patrons. It may even have been Dorothy who recommended to the Red Cross that the organization commission her former boss, Harrison Fisher, to design its promotional posters and advertisements. Yet however happy the pair seemed in public, personally there was a chain of quarrels that culminated in their separation by the summer of 1919.

The question of their marriage's legitimacy, Jules' apathy to the situation, and Clara's constant legal presence were the roots of the discord that propelled them into divorce court in August. There was also the issue of infidelity, nothing new to either of them. While Dorothy found solace in the arms of another man, possibly screen heart-throb Conrad Nagel or German singer Johannes Sembach, who were friends at this time, Jules fell in love with a young, blonde extra girl to whom he had been introduced by collaborator and Eclair alumni Maurice Tourneur. The girl was 19-year-old Texas-born Mae Elizabeth "Hope" Hampton. A beauty contest winner in Philadelphia, where she was raised, Hope danced and sang her way onto the stage, into films and right into Jules' fickle heart. From the background of Tourneur's movies, Brulatour took Hope under his wing to craft her for stardom, just as he had done with Dorothy seven years earlier.

The end of Jules and Dorothy's marriage was a drawn out affair, not concluded until 1923, owing to suits and counter suits, about which not a lot is known. The press, particularly the entertainment media, had a field day with the story, running regular updates on "the matrimonial web that has entangled the Brulatours." The first chapter in their divorce saga opened on August 20, 1919 when Supreme Court Justice Luce refused Dorothy's request for $48,000 in alimony in her pending suit. She was granted $10,000 a year and received, along with that order, a damning moral lecture. As the *New York Times* reported, Luce frankly stated that "the former status of Mrs. Brulatour does not warrant an alimony of $48,000." Interestingly, Jules received no specific reprimand for his behavior in seeking a quick and questionable divorce, which had exposed Dorothy to public humiliation when news was published that their marriage was possibly invalid. Luce did, however, censure both Dorothy and Jules for their "unprincipled conduct in the present case." He said:

> *The papers contain the story of the infidelity of both parties, an utter disregard of marital obligations, and resort by both parties to the court to be relieved of matrimonial vows as if they were nothing more than a mere contract.*

As his statement indicates, the judge also acknowledged during this preliminary examination a counter suit from Brulatour, which charged Dorothy with having been unfaithful. The claim didn't refer to Nagle or Sembach, but did name two other correspondents: Jerome S. Leopold, a prominent New York doctor, and Theodore C. Kanter, a Chicago businessman. Brulatour testified that shortly after marrying Dorothy, he "found her writing a love letter at an early morning hour to another man with whom she confessed she was infatuated." Jules claimed, moreover, that the "other masculine whom she brought into our home" had ended their marriage and "forced him out" of the house. In light of this development, Luce allowed Dorothy, in addition to alimony, some $15,000 in fees to her counsel, one of New

FINDING DOROTHY

York's most prestigious attorneys, Max D. Steuer. In presenting Jules' side of the suit, his counsel simply alleged that

> *the marriage with Mrs. Dorothy Brulatour is void because the divorce [Mr. Brulatour] obtained in Kentucky from his wife, Mrs. Clara Brulatour, in order to marry again, is not binding, as he was not a resident of Kentucky and the court there had no jurisdiction.*

But it was the salacious nature of Brulatour's accusations that enthralled the public. Jules' lawyers not only claimed Dorothy was a scheming "vamp" who had seduced him away from his first wife, but they maintained she had mastermided the quickie divorce. She had, Brulatour testified, "formulated a fraudulent plan to possess herself of my property and force me to support her." He said Dorothy had so manipulated him that he was compelled to "abandon his wife and family to consort with her." And finally, Jules insisted, she "directed the divorce at each and every step," having "studied the divorce laws of various states."

To complicate the scenario, Clara Brulatour's suit to annul Jules' marriage to Dorothy, which had been languishing, was brought to the fore again. He now cooperated in that case, contending that indeed "he was not legally married to his second wife because his divorce was not valid." The autenticity of the marriage wasn't decided for some time, as is shown in immigration forms when both parties, on different occasions, made overseas visits the following year. Dorothy listed herself as married; Brulatour said he was divorced. A litany of lawsuits followed Judge Luce's finding, which was that a strictly valid marriage had not existed between the couple.

A divorce on common-law grounds was granted but Dorothy's alimony was not retracted or reduced. Even so, the outcome of the case humiliated Dorothy to the core. The consequence of subsequent cases, inspired by Luce's ruling, is unclear. The most surprising of these suits was a $50,000 damage claim brought by Dorothy's stepfather, Leonard Gibson, furious at his daughter's ill treatment by Brulatour in seeking a marriage that he probably intended to be a sham from the beginning. The cause of action in Leonard Gibson's case against Jules, filed in New York Supreme Court on May 4, 1920, was not revealed to the press, although much speculation was published. Today, the truth isn't hard to find.

The damages Dorothy's religious father was seeking were for the injury to his daughter's reputation, severely compromised since her affair with Brulatour was exposed in 1913 and compounded considerably on the release of information six years later that their marriage wasn't legal. When asked by journalists about the summons being filed, Gibson's lawyer, Nathaniel Schmidt, "declined to discuss the case at present." The press managed to piece the rest of the story together. Even the generally reticent *Times* went to print with a few flourishes, referring to the ongoing Brulatour divorce and past legal cases, but veered away from giving anything but basic biographical information on Dorothy, who told reporters she wasn't interested in being interviewed.

Meantime, Dorothy retreated to her haven — a small townhouse in the posh Hamilton Hotel complex on W. 73rd Street, where pal Muriel Ostriche was a neighbor. Although officially divorced, problems of alimony and damages pursued Jules, preventing him from

THE AWAKENING

announcing his intention to marry Hope Hampton. As an agent for Hope, Jules actively promoted the new star, setting her up with her own production company and even financing those of her films made by competing studios. Her first starring role, in a movie called *A Modern Salome,* was released to favorable reviews in 1920, the fan magazines waxing enthusiastic over her beauty, hailing her as the screen's "great new personality." But Hope, in spite of a marketable screen presence and apparent acting capability, grew disenchanted with motion pictures, much like Dorothy before her. Motivated by her own ambition or by Jules' influence, Hope would eventually retire from films to make an entry into opera, again closely mirroring the route Dorothy had taken over a decade earlier. Jules' love for Hope, coupled with the attention his prospective bride was getting, made Dorothy understandably depressed.

She was disillusioned to the point of trying to remain friendly with Jules, often socializing with him and Hope at premiers and dinner parties. This state of things persisted until just after Jules and Hope finally married on August 22, 1923. The newlyweds had planned to keep the event a secret for a while longer as Jules was still worried about legal repercussions. But the press was onto them. An interview Brulatour gave to the *New York Times* must have angered Dorothy, knowing well the real reason behind his hesitancy. "We kept it dark because we wanted to be a little different," Jules said. "We thought we would reveal it in one year but it became known, you see. We imagined it would be rather original for a motion picture actress not to make known the fact that she had been married." Sensitive to former mistakes, Brulatour pointed out that he had been living separately from Hope during their courtship.

A further attempt to appear respectable was laughable. "We have been out together constantly," he added, "but we were always chaperoned wherever we went." Dorothy, unwittingly one of their chaperones, was eager to lose the new Brulatours. Trying to be friends with the couple had been a bad idea, and she was soon so upset that her attorney, Max Steuer, convinced her it was best to get out of New York. He recommended she settle in Paris or Rome or some other European city, where her past would not be a liability and she could start her life over. Dorothy spoke of the decision as a release from her turmoil:

> *[After I was divorced] I had a great deal of unhappiness and much less money. Mr. Brulatour had married again, and we still had many of the same friends .... I was not very happy as my husband and his new wife were always around. Therefore I went to Paris to live with my mother .... I already knew Paris very well.... I talked it all over with my lawyer and friend, Max Steuer, and he advised it most strongly. So my mother and I went to Paris.*

Chapter 11:
Miss Masquerader
1924-1938

ALTHOUGH AN ODD AND HAZARDOUS TWIST in their lives would result from their decision to go to France, the move was a natural development for Dorothy and Pauline. Except for the period of the First World War, mother and daughter had visited Paris nearly every year. They didn't enjoy the Atlantic voyages back and forth — being "most timid on the ocean," as Dorothy declared — but they adored Europe. The women especially loved the city of Paris and its people. In fact, as Phillip Gowan has noted, Dorothy soon became "something of a figure in the arts community of Paris." Still good-looking and full of energy in her early thirties, Dorothy, who kept the last name Brulatour despite her divorce, could not have failed to make friends. Most were culled from the expatriate community of artists, musicians, writers and the inevitable political dissidents that gave Paris its special cachet in the 1920s. Her absorption into the latter milieu was to provide excitement for Dorothy over the years, but it would also pose an unforeseeable peril that would threaten her life. Forgetting all about Jules (except when depositing his alimony checks), Dorothy settled into comparative luxury in France, being able to afford niceties which in America would have been prohibitive. "I found the life very cheap and pleasant," she said. "I was happy and content in Paris."

Dorothy and her mother began their Parisian adventure in about 1924 but maintained a Manhattan apartment on West End Avenue for four more years. Aside from entertaining motion picture friends from New York and Hollywood, such as Pearl White, who soon took up residence in Paris as well, and Fannie Ward, who had moved to London, Dorothy recalled meeting literary greats like James Joyce and H.G. Wells. She also came to know the author Colette, whom Dorothy said she "loved and worshipped as a writer and a friend." Another companion of Dorothy's in Paris must have revived memories of her youth — Hugo Fisher, brother of Harrison.

As early as 1922 Dorothy was hobnobbing with the cream of the international set, attending in June a chic recital hosted by the American pianist Leo Tecktonius in his Paris apartment. Among exalted guests were a number of European royals, diplomats and celebrities, from Prince Paul Troubetsskoy, the Grand Duke Boris of Russia and assorted ambassadors to the couturier Lady Duff Gordon, various artists and stage stars. And at a 1924 concert where dancers Harry Pilcer and Florence Walton performed, Dorothy again rubbed shoulders with continental cafe society. Fellow revelers on that occasion included saprano Mary Garden, vaudeville singer Nora Bayes, the Infante Don Luis of Spain, and heiresses Mrs. George Jay Gould and Aimee Crocker Gouraud.

Another glimpse into her social life at this time reveals that Dorothy and her actress pals often threw receptions together, making a farcical theme out of their faded movie careers. "We always have picture parties where Fannie, Pearl and me show our old movies," Dorothy told a reporter for the *Paris Herald*. "It is great fun for us, and for our friends, to watch all those silly escapades and be reminded of the horrid fashions we wore!"

One of their guests was screenwriter Anita Loos whose first novel, the best-selling comedic story *Gentlemen Prefer Blondes,* presented as a diary and illustrated by cartoonist Ralph Barton, was published shortly afterwards. The book, which went on to become a hit play and movie, utilized Fannie Ward and Pearl White as supporting nonsensical characters. But the heroines of the novel were two nit-wit showgirls — Lorelei, a naïve blonde, and Dorothy, a sluttish brunette. It's tempting to infer that the unflattering portrayal of the latter was based on Dorothy Brulatour, whose disastrous marriage was certainly a well-known case study of gentlemen preferring blondes. But there's little concrete evidence, only the obvious parallel and the intriguing circumstance of Anita Loos attending one of Dorothy's "picture parties" while preparing her manuscript.

By 1930, Dorothy had become, as a French society columnist wrote, "one of the smartest women arriving in the capital for the summer season." That year she was spotted by fashion reporters attending the spring collection of Paris designer Lelong. On another occasion in the same salon, wearing an example of the new long skirts that fit tightly over the hips and flared below the knees. Dorothy was accompanied by the Princess Brocatelle and Diane de Rothschild.

Paris may have become Dorothy's spiritual home, but she had yet to make a total break with America. "I went back to New York every year for at least four months," Dorothy recalled. "My taxes were always attended to by Max Steuer and sometimes by my bank." She claimed to have made these annual trips until the outbreak of World War II. But, as Gowan's research shows, Dorothy and Pauline's last extended visit to America was in 1928 and, as historian Don Lynch has found, the last verifiable trip Dorothy made on her own to the U.S. was in 1933. During her visits Dorothy was active socially, attending luncheons and dinner parties that were written up in the society columns of the *New York Post.* Favorite hangouts were the restaurant Sherry's and the club Pierre's. But after 1930 she seems to have cooled toward her American friends.

The conflict between the evidence of researchers and Dorothy's own words suggests clues to the mystery of the Gibsons' erratic lives during this time. For years, Pauline had confined her unorthodox politics to reading and conversation but, finding herself among like minds in the avant-garde set in which her daughter now moved, she was able to support, bodily and financially, the radical causes she cared about. Pauline's views were convoluted but the root of them was apparent hatred for America. This feeling was deep-seated, stemming from the civil rights abuses against Germans she had witnessed during World War I. Pauline came into her own in the realm of subversives to which she attached herself, and these people's effect on her unsettled mind was insidious. Her already forceful personality became more ragged and she started to have manic outbursts of anger.

Dorothy may not have shared her mother's anti-Semitic and Fascist views to the letter but she supported Pauline's involvement in extremist politics. As to the Gibsons' claim that they made regular trips to America until 1939, there's no evidence they did so.

FINDING DOROTHY

"Dorothy alleged yearly trips but that certainly is not true," Gowan has stated, basing his findings on immigration reports and consulate dossiers. "I suspect she was lying to make it less obvious to officials that she had really become an expatriate. She wanted her American passport when it benefited her. Otherwise she wanted nothing to do with the United States." Is it possible Dorothy had forsaken America for the Fascist opinions of her mother and a new circle of dangerous friends? Dorothy could be highly susceptible. It may never be known if there was a sinister dimension to her views, but her loyalties had obviously changed.

When, or why, this turn of mind came about is impossible to pinpoint at this stage, but as Gowan theorizes, the onset of the Great Depression, which caused hardship for Dorothy and her mother in obtaining money from Brulatour and their bank, may have bred "resentment for their native country."

Dorothy, in a letter, does refer pointedly to "the money trouble we had in America" after 1932, adding that "then it would have been a real problem to return to the U.S.A. to live with my mother." Her excuse was that Pauline's "health was not good" and that, as she was in need "of doctors and cures," which were expensive in the States, they would have had a hard time making ends meet there. But might she have been referring to political reasons for not wanting to live in America?

How much the U.S. Government knew about the women's involvement in subversive politics isn't certain, but there is an indication the Gibsons were suspected of being expatriates. "Although both retained United States citizenship," wrote Gowan, "consular officials were frequently involved in obtaining affidavits from the two of them, affirming that they desired the protection afforded American citizens." In some of these affidavits, Dorothy repeatedly stated her unswerving adherence to legalities, sometimes almost childishly, such as when she claimed that she "always exactly followed to the best of my knowledge all rules;" it might have been a line from *Gentlemen Prefer Blondes*. In another report, she felt the need to stress that neither she nor her mother "have ever had French or any other foreign passports." Further clues to the attitude of the Gibsons are contained in statements made in other official documents, which reveal that their ties to family and friends in the States had been severed. Pauline, in one report, confessed that she didn't even know if her sister was still living, not having received word from anyone in America for a "number of years."

Aside from correspondence with her bank in New York and with Brulatour, Dorothy likewise doesn't seem to have kept any American contacts after the early 1930s. The Gibsons' relatives were therefore unaware of their politics or any of their movements in Europe. When Gowan contacted the women's descendants during his research, they told him they had "no hint of (Pauline's) radical political views." Moreover, they were "shocked to learn of them," upon reading copies of the documentation Gowan discovered. The intrigues mother and daughter entered into didn't prevent their enjoying the gracious life of continental society. More than likely, any assignments they undertook required them to socialize and travel. That they were enabling foreign intelligence as enemy operatives hasn't been conclusively proven, but, as Pauline was finally cited for "security violations" and threatened with expulsion to America, and Dorothy would be accused of spying for the Nazis (and for the Allies) and investigated, there seems some validity to the suspicion. One other small, but telling, clue is that although the former actress chose to style herself as Dorothy Brulatour in all official consular and immigration forms, she was generally known as Dorothy Gibson in the right-wing subculture in which she now moved.

If government officials were aware of the Gibsons' activities, the press was not. In 1934, Hollywood journalist Adela Rogers St. Johns, best known for her *Photoplay Magazine* interviews during the silent era, published a series of syndicated newspaper articles on actresses who had retired from movies, focusing on stars "who glimmered but briefly in the orbit of filmdom." St. Johns tracked Dorothy down and, over tea at the Trianon Palace Hotel at Versailles, conducted what is the last known media interview with her. Included with Dorothy in the column series were former *Ziegfeld Follies* showgirl Justine Johnstone and early Essanay Studios leading lady Edna Mayo. These actresses had enjoyed slightly more durable careers in movies than Dorothy, so it's a testament to the impact she must have had on the cinema public of 1911 and '12 that she was remembered at all more than twenty years later. Of her life at the time of the interview, Dorothy, described by the reporter as "pale and pretty in a blue organdie dress and hat," said presciently:

> *Oh my, what a time I am having! I never cared much for motion pictures, you see, and I am too glad to be free of that work. I tell you it was an immense burden. I have had my share of troubles, as you know, but since coming to France, I have recovered from that and feel happy at last. Who could not be deliriously happy in this country? I have such fun. But I fear it cannot go on like this always. I have had my dream life, and am sure that someday a dark cloud will come and wash it all away!*

Coincidentally, on her return to America after meeting Dorothy, St. Johns interviewed another famous *Titanic* survivor, Madeleine Astor Dick, who had recently married Italian prize fighter Enzo Fiermonte. Until 1934, the Gibsons spent each summer at the French resort of St. Jean de Luz. Afterwards the women preferred the beaches of Italy as well as the spas, thermal baths and springs of Tuscany's Montecatini, near Lucca, where they took the "cure." Despite Dorothy's professed concern for her mother's health, her own was possibly worse. By this period she was suffering from severe hypertension with a systolic pressure reaching the alarming level of 260. The annual trips to Montecatini had been prescribed by Dorothy's doctor for its warmer climate; summers there became almost a religious refuge. Unfortunately, these fashionable Italian jaunts didn't help Dorothy much. Now well into her forties, she was beginning to show signs of illness. Yet she was still attractive and charming, if a little overweight, and had no difficulty making the sexual conquests that were so irresistible to her. Dorothy's papers, along with reports from subsequent investigations, bear out that she was as popular as ever with powerful men — the only ones she ever desired. As Gowan found, Dorothy was "romantically involved with a parade of personalities, including diplomats of European countries not entirely friendly with the United States."

At least one serious love affair came out of these dalliances. Dorothy met Emilio Antonio Ramos, chief press attache to the Spanish Embassy in Paris, in about 1932. Spurning his nation's traditional courtship of the *rejah*, Ramos swept Dorothy immediately into a world of government pacts and negotiations, state and royal visits, embassy banquets and, perhaps, high-caliber espionage. As Dorothy's relationship with Antonio Ramos ripened, Pauline relocated to Florence, ostensibly "for treatment by her personal physician," but more likely to be nearer a network of Fascist contacts. This cell would be observed closely by British Special Operations Forces during the dual occupation of Florence by Germany and the Allies in the coming war. Another reason for the separation from Dorothy was Pauline's somewhat strained (and later very acrimonious) relationship with Ramos, who wasn't as tolerant of her fiery temperament as her daughter tried to be. Pauline's idolatry of Mussolini and Hitler also palled on Ramos, who although a neo-Fascist supporter of General Franco, was already leaning to the left in his views. Dorothy remained in Paris but visited her mother regularly, driving her own car, and saw to Pauline's medical care for a condition which was never specified but always alluded to as serious. Dorothy's own health concerned her enough in 1937 for her to update her will, naming Pauline and Antonio Ramos as her beneficiaries. That year, Ramos accompanied Franco's brother, Nicholas, and other delegates representing Nationalist Spain, to the Nazi Party Congress at Nuremberg. Dorothy possibly accompanied her lover to the conference.

While her daughter, as Ramos' acknowledged mistress, was caught up in the glamour of ambassadorial ceremonies in Paris, Pauline was suddenly — and publicly — espousing her increasingly pro-Nazi stance in Florence. Gowan's examination of consular files on Pauline divulged that she

> *began a constant tirade of laudatory comments regarding Nazi concepts and actions that resounded throughout the English and American colony of Florence. She expounded on her hatred of Jews and sympathy with Hitler's goal of a "permanent solution."*

Pauline's views weren't shared by most of her neighbors, who began filing formal complaints about her eccentric behavior. But Pauline was indulged by the authorities for the time being and she continued her rants. When her husband, Leonard Gibson, died in 1938, Pauline barely stopped to notice, leaving his family to carry out funeral arrangements and to settle his estate. Despite her fondness for her stepfather, Dorothy also made no attempt to attend Leonard's funeral or console relatives.

Her life had become a round of parties, and reality seldom interfered with her world. That year her dissipation reached an all-time high when a raucous outing at the Chez Moi nightclub in Florence made the *New York Post*'s gossip page. Dorothy was one of a party that included famous Broadway lyricist Lorenz Hart, New York's Lombardy Club band leader Jimmie Rogers, and two American socialites married to Italian noblemen – Baroness Zezza and the Contessa Contagalli. The *New York Post* reported that Dorothy and her titled chums were "dishing the dirt with Jimmy," and in so doing "got tight as hoot owls." Rogers admitted everyone was drunk: "I lost count after ordering the eighteenth round of champagne." Hart sang songs from his latest show and did an imitation of a bended-knee Al Jolson, belting out "Mammy." Rogers recalled that he and Dorothy "closed the place at 6: 30 a.m.," and met up again the next night to do it all over again.

Chapter 12:
The Lucky Holdup
1938-1944

THE END OF THE ROAD FOR DOROTHY was a thrilling and confusing one. It isn't established to what extent she was engaged in intelligence work, either for France and the Allies or for the Germans in the looming war, but what is known makes the last leg of her journey a tantalizing mystery. For a former entertainment celebrity, now a multimillionaire's divorced wife and a diplomat's expatriate mistress, to add a stint as an American Mata Hari to her repertoire seems fantastic. Yet it might be the truth.

Dorothy had spent a lot of time in Spain throughout 1938, and in 1939 she had an extended stay in Switzerland. The eve of the Second World War found Dorothy in Italy. She had gone with her mother to Alassio where she left her with friends on August 27, 1939, continuing on to Spain, in the company of Antonio Ramos and several others of the Spanish Embassy. Their plans were to come back for their usual cure at Montecatini in a week, spend about a month at that resort and part on October 1, Pauline returning to her villa in Florence and Dorothy going back with Ramos to Paris. But the group was stopped at the border and, as Dorothy recounted in an affidavit, "asked to return to Paris at once."

No one questioned the order and Dorothy accompanied Ramos and his staff back to France. She didn't attempt to collect her mother en route or to communicate the sudden setback to her. Was this strategic? Dorothy must have been aware that war was pending, so why would she leave her mother unless she was certain she was safe? Three days following Dorothy's return to Paris, war was declared. From this point, her behavior seems more puzzling and contradictory. Perhaps it was the realization that her conduct had placed her life in jeopardy and that she was too entrenched to back out. Whatever her thoughts, she now wished to go to Italy and convince Pauline to join her in France. There should have been no convincing necessary. Pauline appears to have been ready to go. Dorothy had had word from her mother to say that she had "gone to Florence, was under the care of the doctor and had asked for a French visa, which was promised but much delayed." It was several months before Dorothy was able to reach her mother. In her own words:

> *Finally I got permission to go to Florence from the American and French governments but to return by a certain time. The winter of 1939 was terrible — cold, rainy, hail — and we had little coal. I found my mother was not very well but was*

FINDING DOROTHY

most comfortable and warm and was being taken care of by the doctor, so I thought it better to leave her there and return to Paris before my permission expired on my passport.

How could it be better to leave one's ailing mother in an enemy country? This question and others can't be answered unless one accepts that the women believed — or hoped — they were under the protection of the Mussolini regime. Dorothy came back to France after visiting her mother, only to return to Italy in the spring of the following year, this time driving her car with the special permission of the French Embassy. She said she made the trip alone that April, which if true, was an incredible risk for a woman in wartime. She would assert that her object was "to get my mother and return." Instead, claiming Pauline "was not well enough to make the trip," she toiled around Florence for ten days, during which time Germany invaded Holland and Belgium. The borders to France now closed, she couldn't return to Paris if she wanted to. Stranded in Italy, Dorothy allegedly made several attempts to secure a visa to go into Portugal and Spain. But these moves were always thwarted by her mother's supposed ill health. So what was really going on? Either the Gibsons were in Florence on a mission, despite their claims, and actually had no interest in fleeing, or else Pauline was resisting her daughter's desire to leave. Whatever the reason, Pauline, sick or not, was immovable from Italy. Judging by her inconsistent behavior, it seems probable at this point that Dorothy was no longer interested in aiding the Fascists and simply wanted out. She was literally running scared. But Pauline would not budge.

Dorothy's plight in Italy was relieved by an eerie distraction when the landmark Hollywood film *Citizen Kane* was released in Europe in late 1941, notable as much for the controversy that occasioned it as for the lauded technical wizardry of its director and star, Orson Welles. The near-harrowing tale of a press magnate's ruthless quest for political power, the movie came too close to home for real-life media king William Randolph Hearst. Alleging *Citizen Kane* defamed him and his mistress, retired silent star Marion Davies, Hearst launched a virtual war against Welles and RKO Pictures, banning any mention of the movie or the studio by his newspaper and magazine empire. What has since struck film historians hit Dorothy like a blow between the eyes when she recognized in *Citizen Kane*'s story more than the obvious references to Hearst. Indeed, the obsessed, Svengali-like character Welles portrayed bore more than a passing resemblance to Jules Brulatour, an angle the press soon made note of and which has since been embraced by modern film scholars.

But what astonished Dorothy most was the movie's merciless characterization of the protagonist's wife in the story, a half-witted, unstable flop of an opera singer who becomes an alcoholic. It was evident this pitiful figure was as much a caricature of herself and Hope Hampton, both pushed into mediocre singing careers by Jules, as it was of the better remembered Davies. In a letter, written years later to friend and fellow journalist Adela Rogers St. Johns, gossip columnist Louella Parsons confirmed that Welles admitted to her that the film was "not so much about Hearst as it was old Brulatour and his sad gals."

THE LUCKY HOLDUP

To have such a major film make a mockery of her disappointments horrified Dorothy. Jules Brulatour, now in his seventies, and Hope were equally unhappy. As for Clara Brulatour, Jules' first wife, she didn't have to endure the insult — she had been killed in a car accident in Cairo some years before, a tragic end to a tragic life. Out of the public eye since her 1919 divorce from Brulatour, Dorothy didn't expect to be reminded of her past in such a dramatic way. Her relationship with Jules had brought her disgrace, but by fleeing to Europe she thought she could live down the stigma of her shame. Dorothy was mistaken. Retirement and anonymity had not been the solution after all, but had permitted a final assault.

Over the next year, mother and daughter "just waited in Italy, hoping things would be better to travel" — a confession which is another discrepancy in Dorothy's papers. Officially she lamented that it was her mother's health that prevented their leaving Italy. Yet in the above excerpt from a letter she avows that it was the political climate that hampered them. What resolve remained with Dorothy disappeared on December 10, 1941. "To my horror," she affirmed, "Mussolini and Hitler declared war on America, a thing I never thought possible …. We were both scheduled to leave by a train provided to evacuate American citizens but were prevented from going by reason of an operation my mother was obliged to undergo, and I had to remain with her." Missing the train to safety, Dorothy was in full panic mode. Her passport was about to expire, and she redoubled efforts to get out of Italy, with or without Pauline. As she recalled:

> *Two days later I wired Rome asking to be taken to America. I was advised I would be taken (by ship). My passport was good until December 20, 1941. I was told to do nothing about my passport. Finally when the boat did not seem ready to leave, I applied for a Swiss protectorate passport. My passports and my money were returned to me, saying it was not necessary as I was being repatriated.*

From what can be gleaned from surviving documents, her repatriation didn't happen, or at least did not come in time to help her. Little is known of the Gibsons' movements for almost two years following December 1941. It seems Dorothy's application for a new passport was either denied or stalled at some point early in 1942. Worried for Dorothy, Antonio Ramos tried to help through various legations, but even he was powerless to save her. Is it possible that she not only didn't have a valid passport during this period but had turned her back on her mother and their Fascist friends by aiding the resistance against the Gestapo, Hitler's secret service? Had she gone into hiding?

A clue to this possibility is the relationship she formed with the young Italian journalist Indro Montanelli. Already well known as a reporter for *Il Corriere della Sera*, Milan's leading newspaper, Montanelli was destined for greater fame as an award-winning political correspondent and freedom fighter. Dorothy first met Montanelli through her erstwhile lover, Ramos, when the former was covering the Spanish Civil War. They continued their friendship in Paris in 1937, after Montanelli was banished from an Italian journalists' union for his objective reporting and exiled temporarily by the National Fascist Party, from which he had resigned. Late in 1943, on receiving permission to return to Italy, Montanelli resumed writing for *Il Corriere*. He also renewed his friendship with Dorothy Brulatour in Florence. Whether the two of them were involved in espionage for the Allies is uncertain. Montanelli,

FINDING DOROTHY

then 34, would later maintain that he was "a spy for nobody;" still, his opposition to the Fascist regime had not lessened and the Questura, or Italian police, kept watch over his movements. As for Dorothy, a consulate report from 1944, containing a statement from her, reveals shattered emotions and what looks like a change of heart:

> *I wish to say that I never wanted to remain in Italy and that I have brought myself nothing but unhappiness and have perhaps completely ruined my life to do the best — as I thought — for my mother.*

Her comments indicate a break in her sympathies with the Fascists, regret of her support of that ideology, possibly even resentment of her mother, whose views had definitely not changed. Dorothy's concern for her safety was paramount on learning that the Questura was regularly monitoring her own activities. Along with befriending Montanelli, Dorothy had begun an affair with an unidentified Florentine nobleman and anti-Fascist, to whom she was engaged, and whom Montanelli recalled was the "real reason she didn't want to leave Italy." She had converted to Catholicism, he claimed, at her fiance's request, despite being a divorcee. Almost nothing concrete is known of this liaison. If the relationship was as important as Montanelli and others said, it may have been formed for political reasons since Dorothy's devotion for Ramos appears to have been genuine.

Dorothy's concern turned to horror when she found that Montanelli had been arrested and imprisoned at the German-controlled Fossoli Concentration Camp near Carpi in Modena. He had written an unflattering article about Benito Mussolini and his mistress Clara Petacci, and the police turned him over to the Gestapo. Soon, the same fate awaited Dorothy's boyfriend, whom Montanelli said "suddenly disappeared in January 1944." Time was clearly running out for Dorothy.

Chapter 13:
Well Protected
1944-1946

THE POLITICAL TURMOIL IN ITALY had increased with the influx of German troops. Insurrections proliferated in Rome, Milan and in villages throughout the country. By September 1943 the Italians, resentful of Hitler's ill treatment of their people, cities and culture, had laid down their arms and declared themselves in support of the Allies. But Germany, still occupying many regions in the country, was hardly willing to pull out. While Allied troops centered their efforts on taking back Rome, pockets of rebels drove out smaller Nazi divisions elsewhere. Even so, most civilian efforts at resistance resulted in their execution or capture by the Germans. As thousands of partisans were killed or sentenced to concentration camps, urban guerillas overtook Fascist leaders and sympathizers wherever they found them. Dorothy and Pauline, steering clear of the mobs that swept through Florence, feared for their safety on learning that politicians and socialites, some probably of their acquaintance, had been assassinated for their indulgence of the Fascists. One of the more famous instances of vigilante tactics was the execution of motion picture stars Osvaldo Valenti and Luisa Ferida, who had allegedly recruited spies for the Nazis. They were in the process of being arrested in Milan when a throng of partisans attacked and shot them on the street.

Though "terribly frightened after the Germans came in," Dorothy remained with Pauline, passing up a final chance to escape to Switzerland. Her explanation was the same; she refused to go without her mother who was too ill to make the journey. Time for flight had expired for Dorothy.

In the first week of April 1944 the Questura informed Dorothy she was being ordered to the Fossoli Concentration Camp. The reason isn't clear. Was she seriously suspected of being in cahoots with partisan rebels in a belated attempt to atone for her former sympathies? Had her association with Indro Montanelli and her mysterious new fiance been discovered? If she knew why the police were after her, Dorothy never confirmed it. Surviving reports are tantalizingly unspecific, classifying her only as an "undesirable" and an "anti-Fascist." Faced with imprisonment at Fossoli, where thousands of patriots were held before being shipped to extermination camps like Auschwitz, Dorothy had no choice but to make a run for the Swiss border without her mother. She felt guilty for leaving Pauline behind. "I would never have left my mother," she said, "and I only tried to escape when it was a question of a camp of concentration." Entrusting Pauline to the care of locals, Dorothy bid her farewell and set off immediately, driving her car as far as she could.

The details of her nightmare trek through Italy, apparently en route to Lucerne, have gone unrecorded. Did friends along the way help Dorothy or did she make the trip un-aided? Now 54 years old and in indifferent health, the experience was arduous as well as terrifying. Dorothy was almost to the border on April 16 when she was captured and arrested by the Nazis at Cernobbio. From there, she was sent immediately to Como and imprisoned. She claimed to have been incarcerated in two more facilities before being removed in mid-May to the political penitentiary of San Vittore in Milan, operated by the Gestapo. The prison to which she was dispatched before being sentenced to San Vittore is believed to have been either that of Bolzano or one of its subsidiary camps, either Merano or Certosa di Val Senales. Bolzano is the most likely as it was known to have had a large number of women political prisoners, many of them radical anti-Fascists or involved with active members of the resistance.

Bolzano was a forced labor camp, based on the German model. Holding up to 3,000 prisoners in ten huts for men and a cell-block for women, the camp was notorious for its appalling conditions, including cases of torture and assassination. On admission, prisoners had their hair shorn and were given uniforms with identification patches. It's estimated that over 11,000 people passed through Bolzano, a great number of these being deported afterwards to Dachau, Auschwitz and other death camps in Germany.

Despite the extreme cruelty of punishment inflicted by the Nazis on prisoners at Bolzano, historians have found that the camp was rife with resistance fighters who braved the risk of execution to maintain close links to outside contacts. This pocket of intelligence perhaps enabled Dorothy to find her way to the physically less harsh but ultimately more dangerous environment of San Vittore. It was there that Dorothy undoubtedly endured untold brutality at the hands of Hitler's state police, infamous for their acts of mental and sexual torture. It was also here that she would embark on the ultimate adventure of her life. Detained with her at San Vittore, she soon found, was her friend Montanelli, who had been sentenced to death while at Fossoli in January but was awaiting a second tribunal hearing. The two communicated somehow despite the danger of discovery by the guards and the fact that they were "chained hand and foot" in different cells. "In San Vittore, it is a living death," Dorothy said. "You can speak to no one — and if you try and are caught the punishment is awful."

But Dorothy, Montanelli (whose new hearing was to no avail) and another prisoner, managed to evolve a plan of escape. Little is known of this third party. His name was General Bortolo Zambon, a 55-year-old former military advisor to the National Liberation Committee whom the Germans had unsuccessfully tried to use as an operative in detecting resistance insurgents in Milan. The trio's hopes were centered on a powerful outsider, a man held in high regard by the Gestapo. His true identity obscured from most people by the bizarre title of "Dr. Ugo," the soft-spoken gentleman was in fact a self-educated Tuscan peasant named Ugo Luca Osteria who had risen in the ranks of governmental intelligence, eventually becoming a secret infiltrator for the Pubblica Sicurezza, using several aliases.

WELL PROTECTED

Now a double agent in the service of Germany and the Allies, Ugo had secured the trust of many in high position. He often conferred with such notables as Cardinal Ildefonso Schuster, Archbishop of Milan, himself a resistance sympathizer, while also wooing one of Hitler's top officers, 30-year-old Kapitan Theodor Saevecke, head of the Gestapo in Milan. Montanelli, learning of Ugo's success in freeing another important prisoner from San Vittore (believed to have been Canadian commando George Paterson), managed to get word to him via the released inmate, as well as through Montanelli's own mother, who made a separate private appeal to Cardinal Schuster. As Dorothy recalled:

> *In San Vittore was an extremely well known man, arrested under a false name. The Germans were, as usual, very stupid and did not know his real name or they would have killed him. Only Dr. Ugo knew him and a friend of mine, also in prison, Indro Montanelli, who had twice been condemned to death. Dr. Ugo saved this man and freed him, and through (his) help Indro Montanelli spoke to Dr. Ugo, and then he persuaded Ugo to call me.*

Dorothy recounted how she learned of the enigmatic special agent who would risk his life in a scheme to save her and her friends:

> *I only heard of (Dr. Ugo) the first part of June, after I had been in prison in Milan about three weeks. I do not know his real name — nobody does — but from what I have seen and heard I can only praise him most highly. His kindness and cleverness have been wonderful. It is difficult to talk to this man .... Dr. Ugo has the right to call people for questioning. After hearing of him it took me nearly a month to get to speak to him.*

What exactly was discussed in her meeting with Ugo in late June 1944? It would seem that the escape strategy he proposed to Montanelli was kept from Dorothy who admitted only to knowing the basic outline when interrogated about it later. She did ask Ugo why he had elected to help her. According to her, he replied "that he was sorry for me as he had never seen anybody look so sick and frightened in his life and, besides that, he liked Americans."

The plan of escape Ugo decided on was elaborately arranged. With the clandestine aid of Cardinal Schuster and a 22-year-old, recently ordained priest named Father Giovanni Barbareschi, he hatched a maneuver to confound the Nazis. By this artifice Ugo, supported by the archbishop and the young priest, informed Kapitan Saevecke in early August that his men had "bungled things terribly" by capturing two of their own spies as well as the agents' accomplice and financial backer, "an American millionairess."

As Barbareschi would recall, Dorothy was also described by Ugo to the Gestapo as a "niece of President Franklin Roosevelt and the fiancee of an Italian aristocrat" (confirming Montanelli's recollection that she was involved with "an old count"). The former

FINDING DOROTHY

claim was certainly a fabrication, though it could have been a ploy authorized by Office of Strategic Services agent Kermit Roosevelt (grandson to Theodore) who was active in assisting the resistance in Northern Italy in 1944; he may even have been part of the San Vittore escape plot. Australian Lieutenant John Desmond Peck, who was aiding partisan cells in Milan at this time, may also have been involved.

At any rate, Ugo advised the police to release the three captives as soon as possible as the Allies, having taken Rome, were advancing on Milan. The operatives, he insisted, must be allowed to enter Switzerland for the protection of valuable military secrets and to carry out further duties. Both Barbareschi and Montanelli remembered that Ugo continually referred to Dorothy in his appeals as "a precious exchange commodity."

Coupled with the archbishop's suggestion that it was "well to facilitate the exodus from San Vittore of these important persons," Ugo finally convinced Saevecke to comply with the request. On Monday, August 14, the Gestapo head ordered an "armored vehicle" (according to Montanelli) to drive the discharged prisoners to the Swiss border. Barbareschi recalled a different scenario. He said he was under the impression that Saevecke had not yet approved the release of the prisoners but had agreed to allow them a short visit with Ugo at the nearby Hotel Regina, where the SS interrogation station was set up. He learned later that Saevecke had unofficially cooperated with Ugo in the release of Dorothy, Montanelli, and Zambon as part of a bargain to "gain merits" with undisclosed intelligence sources. Barbareschi said Ugo devised the interval of transportation between the prison and hotel as the ideal moment of escape.

He further stated that Ugo's own car was the getaway vehicle and that the mysterious emissary himself drove the prisoners directly from the jail to the border. Barbareschi admitted that he, too, "accompanied the group to the border personally" and was honored to accomplish such a "deed of fraternal mercy." Although wearing his clerical cassock, Barbareschi, a chaplain in the partisan association Fiamme Verdi, introduced himself to Dorothy and the others during the flight to Switzerland only as "Don Paolo," the code name he used when engaged in resistance work. Barbareschi, who is now in his nineties and still active in his parish in Milan, said he was proud of his efforts to overthrow the Nazis and didn't worry about the danger of his role in the scheme to free Dorothy and her friends. "Consider that I was 22 years old at the time," he said modestly, "and what everyone calls heroic deeds were normal actions for young people. Although the risk was really great, I felt a deep need to help prosecuted politicians and my Jewish brothers, and to continue on the path to spread the values of liberty and democracy."

As the vehicle driven by Ugo approached the outskirts of Milan, Barbareschi became aware that their frightened companions, whom he recalled were "in pitiful condition," were not completely convinced they were "travelling towards freedom." When assurances were made, he recalled that Dorothy appeared "deeply moved." He didn't remember much conversation on the journey that day. "For the whole way, we kept very silent," he said. Asked in 2005 why he risked his life to aid these three forlorn strangers, Barbareschi replied, "When the freedom of a person is in danger, one is morally obliged to do everything possible to help him." When interviewed, he also said he did not consider them to be strangers; they were "our friends." At the edge of town, the car was stopped at a German check point for what must have seemed an interminable time. Documents, including a pass bearing

WELL PROTECTED

Saevecke's forged signature (made from a stamp obtained by Barbareschi) was presented to the station guards. As one officer examined the papers, another peered into the vehicle. At last, the guard handed the documents back to Dr. Ugo and waved him through the gate.

The big car lumbered across the countryside, passing through the towns of Varese, Malnate, Cagno and Uggiate. In the early evening hours of August 14, at the tiny border village of Ronago, Ugo stopped in front of an old farmhouse. Barbareschi asked Dorothy, Montanelli and Zambon to join him for a visit with his friend and "tested collaborator," Mrs. Palmiro Ambrosoli, owner of the namesake caramel factory. She met the group, accompanied by her companion, known to Barbareschi only as Miss Lydia. Both ladies, he said, had "proven themselves faithful through the most delicate and difficult passages." The otherwise nondescript little house, which sat squarely on the Swiss border, had apparently served many on their escape to freedom. But each attempt was potentially hazardous in a town occupied by Germans. Fortunately the border patrol, while subject to Nazi orders, was composed mainly of officers who were anti-Hitler/anti-Mussolini partisans.

Mrs. Ambrosoli and Miss Lydia had succeeded in infiltrating the local patrol to gain accomplices in their underground efforts to help Jews and other political prisoners reach the safety of the Swiss station of Novazzano, only a mile or so away. The way to freedom for the prisoners would be gained at the foot of a meadow where the grass arched into a small knoll; Montanelli called it "the blessed little hill that separated oppression and liberty." At sunset Ugo, his young accomplice and the three prisoners, together with their hostesses, set out across the field. They walked "all arm in arm," Barbareschi recalled, the gesture providing a signal to a friendly border patrol guard, posted nearby, to "look away." As the group passed within sight of a watch tower, Barabareschi still remembers with emotion that the officer on duty didn't turn his back as usual but "saluted us and smiled." Once over "the blessed hill" of safety, euphoria overtook Zambon. The general ran for cover behind "a stretch of rocky hills," remembered Montanelli, who followed closely behind. But for Dorothy, feminine good manners took precedence over danger and before joining her friends on their hike to freedom, she thanked her liberators for their heroism "through a stream of tears."

The priest remembers the special parting words she reserved for him: "God has saved my soul," Dorothy told Barbareschi in a wavering voice, "and you have saved my life." The young cleric was affected by the sentiment as he watched the frail woman scurry into the gathering shadows. Although Barbareschi would come to know Montanelli in later years, he never saw the mysterious American lady again. But he hasn't forgotten the graciousness she showed in the midst of fear on that memorable summer night. Before starting back over the hill, Ugo, Barbareschi and the two women waited for a quarter of an hour, "the time necessary for our friends to reach Navazzano." When they turned around, the group walked single-file and "no longer arm in arm." According to Barbareschi, this was the signal of "mission accomplished" to the border guard, who, pretending "not to notice there were three missing." saluted again and smiled.

FINDING DOROTHY

In the wake of the trio's escape, the U.S. Army took Milan. Dorothy, Montanelli and Zambon were lucky to get away when they did; the Germans would have executed them before allowing them to fall into enemy hands. In Dorothy's words, the man she officially knew only as Dr. Ugo

> *freed me, telling all lies to the Germans. To this day, I do not know what all his lies were, but something to the effect that a General Zambone (sic), who escaped with us, and Montanelli were to be spies and I was to help with money. Dr. Ugo told Zambone, Montanelli and me to speak to our governments in Switzerland immediately and tell them all the truth. He asked us to refrain from giving any story to a newspaper until the Americans and English were in Milan.*

Once in Switzerland, Dorothy, Zambon and Montanelli struck out from Navazzano through the Alps and over the Rhone River for the city of Bern where they were detained and their papers seized by the police.

The Italian and American embassies in Zurich were then informed by the authorities of the presence of the two men and a woman who claimed to have escaped from San Vittore. An investigation was ordered and the three were transported to Zurich to appeal to their consuls. At the American Embassy, Dorothy was ushered into the office of Vice Consul-General James C. Bell. She made a sympathetic impression on Bell who, while assuring her that he felt she was innocent, explained that a thorough inquiry would have to be conducted before her release could be secured. Of the allegations that she was a spy, he claimed Dorothy "was greatly alarmed when we informed her of these suspicions." Bell asked her to submit a short affidavit, detailing her activities during the war and her reasons for remaining in a Nazi-occupied territory. She completed the form and was taken away by the police. Montanelli and Zambon underwent the same procedure at the Italian Consulate.

Pending the outcome of their cases, the group was confined to separate detention camps. Dorothy remembered being interned at two camps before being admitted to the San Rocco Clinic at Lugano, uncomfortably near the Italian border. From Lugano, she was finally able to communicate by phone and telegram with Ramos in Paris and her mother in Florence, telling them of her unbelievable escape from the Gestapo. In the meantime, she learned from Montanelli that he and Zambon had been cleared by their embassy's inquest and were "both awaiting instructions to return to help the 5th Army." While there, she also heard of the misfortune that had befallen her benefactor, the shadowy Dr. Ugo. She was told that a priest associated with Cardinal Schuster — this was not Barbareschi — and another double agent by the name of Valerio Benuzzi, had

> *denounced (Ugo) to the Germans for the joke he had played on them — that the general, journalist and American were here in Switzerland and were not spies.*

As a later intelligence report filed by Theodor Saevecke revealed, his informants claimed that Dr. Ugo planned to undermine the Germans through an elaborate scheme that on the surface seemed to benefit the Nazis, but would actually ensnare them. Saevecke maintained that Ugo had hoped to penetrate Allied intelligence rings in Switzerland, the plan involving

WELL PROTECTED

the employment of Montanelli, Dorothy, and Zambon. The three were to be released, ostensibly through the influence of Ugo, and conducted into Switzerland. When they were there, Ugo was to enter Switzerland himself, pose as their liberator and as an enemy of Germany, and state his willingness to work for the Allies.

According to Saevecke's sources and the doctor's own confession, when eventually captured by the Allies, Ugo wanted the Nazis to think the intelligence collected by the three "spies" would aid Germany's fight against liberation forces in Italy, while in fact any information obtained was to benefit the invading Allies. Neither story can be proved or disproved. It's just as likely there was no espionage involved one way or the other, and that it was all a prevarication to get the three to safety. Ugo convinced Saevecke for the time being that he was innocent of any conspiracy, but he knew he was in danger and fled as soon as he could, managing to get to Switzerland where British Special Operations Forces apprehended him.

On the other hand, there's some evidence that Saevecke himself may have been secretly in cahoots with the Allies on some level during this period; documents show he was definitely in contact with OSS operative and future head of the CIA, Kermit Roosevelt. Following the war, the CIA actually employed Saevecke as an agent planted in the West German criminal police service. This information tends to support the possibility that the OSS was in on the escape plan to free Dorothy. It certainly would explain the ruse she used that she was related to President Roosevelt.

Dorothy felt badly for Ugo for the "great deal of trouble" in which he found himself after masterminding her escape. "He has earned my eternal gratitude," she said. As for the involvement of Cardinal Schuster and Father Barbareschi, Dorothy likely never realized the pivotal role they played in her release. Montanelli himself would not discover the lucky connivance of the heroic prelates until nearly a decade later. Dorothy also had no idea that the young priest was himself soon to be incarcerated at San Vittore, having been arrested by the Gestapo for helping a Jewish family flee from a deportation order. After two months of torturous interrogation and "not being able to see the starry sky," Barbareschi's freedom was secured through the intervention of Cardinal Schuster. The archbishop summoned the young man to his office on his release and, before his staff and visitors, knelt and kissed his hands. "What you are doing is right," Schuster told Barbareschi. "Carry on."

Dorothy's release from internment was finally obtained in the fall of 1944 after Vice-Consul Bell in Zurich received a longer, more detailed affidavit from her in Lugano. He concluded she was not guilty of espionage as "the accused hardly seems bright enough to be useful in such capacity." Perhaps, that was where her brightness came in. On leaving the San Rocco Clinic, she was persuaded by a friend to remain in Switzerland for a few months in order to recuperate from the hardship of the last staggering year. Dorothy's health hadn't been good for a long time, and the starvation and abuse she had endured while imprisoned in Italy had exacerbated her condition.

But as soon as France was liberated from the Nazis, Dorothy rushed back to Paris, her beautiful apartment in the Hotel Ritz, and the arms of her lover. And what of Dorothy's

FINDING DOROTHY

aged and ill mother? "Dorothy was able to visit Pauline as the war was winding down," noted Phillip Gowan in his 2002 study of the women, "but she chose to live in Paris while her mother remained in Florence .... The two always professed total love and loyalty for one another, and the allegations against Dorothy were put to rest once and for all." That is not to say that Pauline's political loyalties ever changed, which may be the reason for the friendly distance her daughter now chose to keep. Dorothy's concern for her mother remained, but her indulgence of Pauline's radical beliefs had seen its day. "I do not comprehend her at times," she confessed to Montanelli.

Still suffering from high blood pressure, Dorothy was admitted to the American Hospital in Paris at Neuilly early in 1945 and treated for "valvular heart disease and hypertension." She chose to convalesce at the Swiss resort of Vevey, joined by Ramos, throughout the summer and early autumn of that year, writing friends, including Montanelli, that she was "gorgeously happy." Spent with the man she loved, that idyllic summer on Switzerland's Lake Geneva was her last. Lolling in the sun among the flowers in the land where her life had been spared, Dorothy's thoughts wandered back over the years. She had felt great love and suffered greater loss, made appalling mistakes and noble amends, been rich as well as deprived, witnessed tragic death and precious salvation. She hadn't experienced the bliss she had dreamt of in marriage, having children or living in the country. But she had found peace.

When she came back to Paris at the end of 1945, the war was over and so were all her worries. Dorothy expected to "return to life," as she told Montanelli, "to start afresh." She didn't know she had come back to say goodbye. The beautiful city that had delivered her from despair after Jules went out of her world would be the scene of her last hours. Her life had almost seen its end in the icy waters of the North Atlantic, had again hung in the balance in a decrepit Italian war prison. But fate allowed Dorothy Gibson Brulatour to bid farewell amid the gilt grandeur of the Ritz Hotel. Europe's most elegant accommodation, its Edwardian heyday had coincided with her own. When Dorothy fell dead from a heart attack in her suite on the morning of February 17, 1946, she was still gorgeously happy. She had let go her dreams of Julie and Mutsie, of the desire to understand her mother, of the pain the *Titanic* had wrought, of the horror of her political blunders. The past no longer hurt. She was free.

Epilogue

DOROTHY'S DEATH WENT ALMOST unnoticed by the world's press. The public had long for-gotten the Harrison Fisher Girl and silver screen comedienne. Even her fame as a *Titanic* survivor meant little to a generation that had witnessed the Holocaust and Hiroshima. Family and friends remembered Dorothy for her funny, energetic personality. But nobody else seemed even to know her name. Certainly almost no one beyond a few Hollywood insiders and her intimate circle knew that the infamous character of Susan Alexander in *Citizen Kane* was partly based on her. Fewer still were aware of her chilling experiences behind enemy lines as an alleged spy, although that role was destined for the screen as well. Her old friend Indro Montanelli had written a best-selling novel, *Generale Della Rovere*, based on the ad-venture of his escape from San Vittore. Dorothy was portrayed in the book as a woman in-volved with a high-ranking official who had been captured by the Nazis. Director Roberto Rossellini turned the book into a widely acclaimed, award winning film in 1959. With Mon-tanelli penning the movie's script as well, Dorothy was the basis of the character of Mme. Fassio, who schemes for the release of her lover.

When asked many years later by journalist Eduardo Mata about the true identities of the fictional characters in his book and screenplay, Montanelli wouldn't mention names at first. Yet he admitted that the Mme. Fassio figure in his tale was based on "an expatriate American actress of motion pictures" who had a "politically naive mother" and a "boyfriend jailed by the Gestapo." Montanelli was asked if any of the others he was with in prison (whom he finally did identify) were really spies. He said none of them were spies but that they all had "big hearts in the wrong places" and were "very gullible." He added – perhaps unfairly – that Dorothy, in particular, was "stupid as a goat."

Now, 65 years since her death, there isn't one person in a thousand who has ever heard of Dorothy Gibson. It's almost as if her fame as an artist's model and actress in silent pictures never occurred. But she isn't totally forgotten. Today there are Internet pages de-voted to Dorothy; an exquisitely detailed Dorothy Gibson doll is even available for online purchase, designed by Alice Leverett. *Harrisonfisher.com*, a popular Website that pays trib-ute to the artist's life and work, features a number of his illustrations of Dorothy. What's more, the increasing collectors' market for the artwork of Harrison Fisher has produced a network of aficionados and scholars who covet the minutia of the illustrator's life and career. Dorothy is known and appreciated by many serious Fisher fans, even though facts about her tenure with him are scanty. Currently, original postcards and prints of his images of her are among the most expensive to acquire as are Fisher's magazine covers of her. An in-

FINDING DOROTHY

scribed copy of his 1911 book, *American Belles*, containing the largest number of identifiable Dorothy paintings, recently reached an all-time market value of $2,300.

In the arena of film history, a newfound appreciation of long-forgotten stars has begun as those in the vanguard of silent cinema scholarship reassess the contributions of pioneering actors like Dorothy, and much that is new may be forthcoming from these researchers. Presently, the importance of Dorothy Gibson in movie history is relegated to her most famous role (that of herself) in 1912's *Saved From the Titanic*. From a cultural standpoint, the picture is considered by film historian Frank Thompson to be one of the most significant losses of the silent era. Meantime, a movement to celebrate the vital impact of the studios, filmmakers and stars of Fort Lee on the history of American motion pictures promises to resurrect interest in that trailblazing mecca from which sprung the modern Hollywood system. Within this context, Dorothy stands a chance at rediscovery, even if only as a byproduct of new information coming to light on Éclair or Jules Brulatour, two Fort Lee mainstays and each central to the evolution of American movies.

And with the resurfacing of the film *The Lucky Holdup*, Dorothy may be on her way to being reclaimed. Although one of her minor roles, the picture's restoration provides the first glimpse modern audiences have had of the enigmatic star. Her sweet smile, that naughty look out of her eyes, and her ability to use those expressions with precision on film can now be appreciated. And they have been. In November 2004, the first public screening of *The Lucky Holdup* since its original release was held at the St. Louis Film Festival.

Finally, the resurgence of popular interest in the *Titanic* disaster in the last half century (but especially since the 1997 blockbuster film by James Cameron), has assured for Dorothy Gibson a special place in the hearts of liner buffs. Even after Phillip Gowan's unveiling of the star's darker side in his expose for the British Titanic Society's quarterly journal, the *Atlantic Daily Bulletin*, Dorothy has continued to fascinate readers and Web-surfers into the 21st century.

Living memory of Dorothy is practically nonexistent. The last person alive who actually knew her is probably Father Giovanni Barbareschi, the brave cleric who helped her escape execution at San Vittore. Still preaching in the Italy he loves, Barbareschi is now an elderly man, but his memories of his youth as a resistance fighter are vivid. Dorothy was a shattered woman when she made the fateful acquaintance of the young priest from Brescia, but her liberator saw in her "a spirit of hope," all the more radiant in that most perilous moment of her life.

Apart from books, articles, images and archival documents, there's little other tangible evidence of Dorothy's life. The downtown Hoboken church in which her mother and stepfather married, and in which she was baptized, still stands on Bloomfield Street, now serving a Seventh Day Adventist congregation. Its Romanesque revival architecture seems out of place among modern minivans and power lines but it's still there. Her swank Riverside Drive penthouse didn't survive the wrecking ball of progress. Neither did her Paris apartment. But the Brulatour Building, erected by her former husband, still faces Fort Lee's Jane Street, a monument as much to his one-time love for Dorothy as to his devotion to filmmaking.

There are few other landmarks left but they're poignant ones. Some ramparts of the grim Milanese prison of San Vittore, where Dorothy cheated death, still stand and a few

EPILOGUE

dilapidated buildings of the Fossoli Camp, to which she was once sentenced, are being restored as reminders of the Holocaust. There is also the vessel *Nomadic*, the former White Star Line tender that ferried Dorothy and her mother out to the *Titanic* from Cherbourg in the dusk of 100 Aprils ago. The boat is now a maritime memorial in Belfast.

And the *Titanic* itself, aboard which a carefree Dorothy dreamt of the man she adored, rests majestically in the swirling shadows of the deep. Dorothy's memory is inextricably bound to the haunted wreck, so much so that her image seems stuck in time, as frozen in 1912 as the iceberg that overwhelmed the great ship, the lives of 1,500 people, and a world that's never forgotten the loss. Not only historically but cinematically, Dorothy remains in a kind of void. Her only surviving film premiered just as the *Titanic* set sail, ensuring that people see her now as she was at the height of her fame — beautiful, happy, full of life and love.

But the most intimate physical connection to Dorothy's story is the place where her journey ended in 1946. From an early age Dorothy had fantasized a bucolic retreat for herself, a dream never fulfilled. But what she didn't get in life she has found in death. Her final resting place is an old cemetery on the outskirts of Paris, in the picturesque country village of Saint Germain-en-Laye. Interred with her is her mother, who survived Dorothy by fifteen years. Their mutual grave, shaded by a tree's broad canopy, overlooks a serene valley that leads to the eternally rolling Seine.

Acknowledgments

EVERY PROJECT HAS its guardian angel. We're proud to say this one had six. Without the involvement of these individuals, there would have been no story to tell. The contributions they made were key not only to finding Dorothy but to appreciating her to the full.

To our original publisher and patroness extraordinaire, Carolyn Byars (always a phone call and a credit card away!) goes our sincerest gratitude. She was much more than our financial backbone. She was our cheerleader and savior. Whatever the roadblock, she got us through. No one has had greater faith in us or in the power of this story than Carolyn, and we salute her for her dedication, energy, inspiration and friendship.

Our thanks are also extended to historian and biographer Phillip Gowan, who supplied several photos of Dorothy Gibson that appear in these pages and upon whose research much of our information about her later life was based. Both his findings and extensive collection of images were crucial. Without the precedent of his illuminating work and his courteous sharing of the fruits of that study, this undertaking would not have been possible.

Collector Jean Collins' little eBay find of a scrapbook that had once belonged to artist Harrison Fisher has yielded such treasures and proved so essential to us that thanking its generous owner in a few lines seems inadequate. Jean's amazing kindness and diligence in making photocopies and transcripts available to us from this fragile volume of news clippings about Dorothy and other Fisher models can never be repaid.

The same goes for Marsha Buckley, whose once discarded file of manuscripts, letters and articles belonging to reporter Adela Rogers St. Johns, proved an invaluable source. The answer to many riddles came from St. Johns' notes for her published and unpublished stories on Dorothy Gibson. Throughout our book, many of the personal quotes from Dorothy, revealing her thoughts and observations, owe their existence to Buckley for preserving the St. Johns collection which she found in an industrial waste bin in Oakland, California in 1987.

A similar chance discovery of *The Lucky Holdup*, the only Dorothy Gibson film known to exist, infused an unexpected thrill into this project. Finally being able to assess Dorothy's screen persona in this rare movie, salvaged by David Navone in 2001 from an abandoned storage locker in Bakersville, California, was a dream come true. We can never thank him enough for his heroism in rescuing Dorothy's moving image and for giving us permission to experience it for ourselves.

Finally, to Don Giovanni Barbareschi, probably the last person alive who actually knew Dorothy Gibson, we owe our deepest appreciation and thankfulness for recalling the

ACKNOWLEDGMENTS

extraordinary mission he facilitated to free her from prison at San Vittore in 1944. In addition to the photos, articles and notes Father Barbareschi shared, the touch of living memory he gave to this book has enriched it tremendously.

Apart from these essential sources, many more people have contributed unique elements. Film historians Frank Thompson, Dr. Paolo Cherchi Usai, Marc Wanamaker, Professor Richard Koszarski, Greta de Groat, Leslie Midkiff de Bauche and Q. David Bowers supplied rare photographs, information and much appreciated advice and support. A special thank you goes out to Tom Meyers, executive director of the Fort Lee Film Commission, and to collectors Stephen Dodd and Benjamin Tierney for sharing their expertise.

Library of Congress librarians and researchers deserve praise for going well beyond the call of duty. Kathryn Blackwell of the Prints and Photographs Division, Rosemary Hanes of the Motion Picture, Broadcasting and Recorded Sound Division, Bonnie Coles of the Photoduplication Service, and Jerry Hatfield of the Public Services Office each guided us to exciting discoveries.

We also want to single out the efforts of Kim Tomadjoglou, curator of the American Film Institute; Janet Lorenz of the National Film Information Service; Donna Chong of Madison Press; Rita Altamara of the Fort Lee Public Library; Ray Lowry of the Ennis Public Library; the staff of the Fine Arts Department of the Dallas Public Library; Don Raffaelo Farina of the Vatican Library; Rev. Mons. Bruno Bostra of the Archives of the Diocese of Milan; and Don Mirko Bellora of the parish of S. Maria del Suffragio.

The following agencies, archives and libraries were also helpful: the Margaret Herrick Library at the Academy of Motion Picture Arts and Sciences; the Shubert Archive; the University of Texas at Austin; the Billy Rose Theatre Collection at the New York Public Library for the Performing Arts; the Museum of Modern Art; George Eastman House; the AFI.com web team; Adam Matthew Publications Ltd; and Butterfield and Butterfield Auctioneers (formerly Dunning's).

In the world of *Titanic* research we are happy to thank author George Behe for loaning beautiful photographs from his amazing private collection and for offering valuable advice. We're also indebted to the generosity of historian Don Lynch, painter Ken Marschall and his company, Trans-Atlantic Designs, Geoff Whitfield, treasurer of the British Titanic Society, and Robert Rydell Shotton and Olivier Mendez of the Association Francaise du Titanic. Other experts in the realm of Titanica to whom we owe thanks are Philip Hind, editor of *Encyclopedia-Titanica.org,* Michael Tennaro, editor of *TitanicBookSite.com*, trustee for the Titanic International Society, Shelley Dziedzic, and writer-researchers Pat Cook, Jenni Atkinson, Ben Holme, Daniel Klistorner, Bill Wormstedt, Monica Hall and Inger Sheil.

A debt of thanks is in order as well to Kalman and Eva Tanito and Zsolt Mihok for their efforts in translating Italian documents and letters; to Eduardo Mata for making copies of letters available to us from Indro Montanelli as well as a transcript of his 1978 taped interview with Montanelli; to Karl Benson for sending us a copy of his unpublished essay on Jules Brulatour; to Victoria Alvarez for sharing her thesis on the Shubert Brothers; to Linda Kelly for selling us photographs and postcards from her collection; to Alice Leverett for permission to use a photo of her Dorothy Gibson doll; to Averyl Hill for use of information and images from her website, *Harrisonfisher.com*; to Jonathan Whitney for his photograph of the former First Baptist Church of Hoboken, New Jersey; and to Michael and Laurie

FINDING DOROTHY

Wilson for their friendship.

Lastly we want to thank graphic designer Arlene Honza for her technical advice, Susie J. Wilson for her PR help, our friend Donna Smith for her support, and our families for their love and understanding.

Bibliography

History of Theatre and Film

Allen, Jeanne, "The Decay of the Motion Picture Patents Company," *Cinema Journal,* Spring 1971, vol. 10, pp. 34-40.

Alpert, Hollis, *Broadway: 125 Years of Musical Theatre*, New York: Little, Brown and Co., 1991.

Baral, Robert, *Revue: The Great Broadway Period,* New York: Fleet Press Corp., 1962.

Billboard, "The History of Motion Pictures," February 3, 1912, p. 4ff.

Blum, Daniel, *A Pictorial History of the Silent Screen,* New York: Gossett and Dunlap, 1972.

_____. *A Pictorial History of the American Theatre,* New York: Greenberg Publishers, 1950.

Bowser, Eileen, *The History of the American Cinema: The Transformation of Cinema, 1907-1915, Vol. II,* Berkeley: University of California, 1994.

Clarke, Daniel B., "A Mid-Year Cinematograph Review," *American Cinematographer,* June 1926, p. 12.

D'Agostino, Annette M., *Filmmakers in The Moving Picture World: An Index of Articles, 1907-1927,* Jefferson, NC: McFarland & Co., 1997.

De Bauche, Leslie Midkiff, *Reel Patriotism: The Movies and World War I,* Madison, Wisconsin: University of Wisconsin Press, 1997.

Green, Abel, and Laurie, Joe, *Showbiz: From Vaude to Video,* New York: Henry Holt and Co., 1951.

Griffith, Richard, and Mayer, Arthur, *The Movies,* New York: Simon and Schuster, 1970.

Griffithiana, "The Eclair Film Company," 1992 Vol. 44/45, pp. 5-14 .

_____. "The Eclair Trademark from Nick Carter to Zigomar," 1993 Vol. 47.

Karney, Robyn, Ed., *Cinema Year by Year (1894-2000),* New York: Dorling Kindersley, 2000.

Koszarski, Richard, *Fort Lee: The Film Town (1904-2004),* Indiana: University of Indiana Press, 2004.

Lauritzen, Einar and Lundquist, Gunnar, *American Film Index, 1908-1915.* Stockholm: University of Stockholm, 1976.

Musson, Bennett, "Fortunes in Films," *McClure's,* November 1912, pp. 65-76.

Rapee, Erno, *The Encyclopedia of Music for Pictures,* New York: Belwin, 1925.

Richardson, F.H., "Projection Department," *Moving Picture World,* Dec. 2, 1911, p. 721-

722.
Slide, Anthony, *The American Film Industry: A Historical Dictionary,* New York: Lime light Editions, 1990.
Tarbox, Charles H., *Lost Films 1895-1917,* Los Angeles, Film Classic Exchange, 1983.
Thompson, Frank, *Lost Films: Important Movies That Disappeared,* New York: Carol Publishing Group, 1996.
Usai, Paolo Cherchi, *The Death of Cinema: History, Cultural Memory and the Digital Dark Age,* London: The British Film Institute, 2001.
_____. *Burning Passions: An Introduction to the Study of Silent Film,* London: The British Film Institute, 1994.
Van Zile, Edward S., *That Marvel the Movie,* New York: G.P. Putnam's Sons, 1923.

Harrison Fisher
Andrews, Barbara, "Harrison Fisher: A Cynic About Women?" *Antique Trader Weekly,* May 11, 1976.
Bowers, Q. David, *Harrison Fisher,* Wolfeboro, NH, Bowers, 1985.
Brissard, Evelyn, "A New Harrison Fisher Girl: Miss Dorothy Gibson," *New York Sunday American,* undated (circa 1909), Marsha Buckley Collection.
Cosmopolitan, "Father of a Thousand Girls," June 1910, pp. 135-36.
Cortlandt, Roberta, "Harrison Fisher Girls Tell Their Stories," The *New York Morning Telegraph,* undated (circa 1911), Marsha Buckley Collection.
Fisher, Harrison, *A Garden of Girls,* New York: Dodd, Mead, 1910.
_____. *American Belles,* New York: Dodd, Mead, 1911.
_____. *Beauties,* New York: Dodd, Mead, 1913.
_____."The Psychology of Dress," *Dress Magazine,* p.6.
"Harrison Fisher's Beauty Ideals," *New York American,* undated (circa 1911), Marsha Buckley Collection.
The Ladies' Home Journal, "The Creator of the Harrison Fisher Girl," February 1910.
The New York Herald, "Mr. Fisher Believes in Every Woman's Beauty," undated (circa 1911), Marsha Buckley Collection.
The New York Times, "Harrison Fisher Discovered a New Type of Beauty," January 22, 1911.
Skinner, Tina, *Harrison Fisher: Defining the American Beauty,* Atglen, PA: Schiffer Publishing Ltd., 1999.
Welch, Naomi, *The Complete Works of Harrison Fisher, Illustrator,* La Selva Beach, CA: Images of the Past, 1993.
_____. *American and European Postcards of Harrison Fisher, Illustrator,* La Selva Beach, CA: Images of the Past, 1999.

Personalities
Barbareschi, Giovanni, "Montanelli In Fuga da S. Vittore Verso la Liberta", *Il Segno,* October 2001, p. 38-40.
Bowers, Q. David, *Muriel Ostriche: Princess of Silent Films,* New York: Vestal Press, 1987.

BIBLIOGRAPHY

Brady, Frank, *Citizen Welles: A Biography of Orson Welles,* New York: Scribners, 1987.

Brunette, Peter, *Roberto Rosselini,* New York: Oxford University Press, 1987.

Kael, Pauline, *Raising Kane: The Citizen Kane Book,* New York: Bantam, 1971.

New York Dramatic Mirror, "Jules Brulatour: President of the Motion Picture Distributing and Sales Company," January 31, 1912, p. 51.

The Moving Picture World, "Famous Director for the Independents (Etienne Arnaud)," December 30, 1911, p. 1079.

_____. "Lamar Johnstone (Obituary)," June 14, 1919, p. 1631.

_____. "Putting it Over Us (Harry Raver)," October 1, 1910, p. 758.

_____. "Carl Laemmle Talks to Us," May 22, 1909, p. 673.

_____. "The Motion Picture Distributing and Sales Company (Jules Brulatour and Carl Laemmle)," April 16, 1910, p. 595.

_____. "The Cradle of the Moving Picture (George Eastman)," August 7, 1909, pp. 190-91.

Pizzitola, Louis, *Hearst Over Hollywood: Power, Passion and Propaganda in the Movies,* New York: Columbia University Press, 2002.

Sloper, William T., *The Life and Times of Andrew Jackson Sloper,* privately printed, 1949.

Titanic

Bottomore, Stephen, *The Titanic and Silent Cinema,* London: The Projection Box, 2000.

Eaton, John P., "*Titanic* in Films: Liner's Story Inspires Early Cinematic Productions," *Voyage,* June 1991, (Vol. 8), pp. 151-161.

Lord, Walter, *A Night to Remember,* New York: Holt, Rinehart and Winston, 1955.

Lynch, Don, and Marschall, Ken, *Titanic: An Illustrated History,* Toronto: Madison Press, 1992.

McMillan, Beverly, and Lehrer, Stanley, *Titanic: Fortune and Fate,* New York: Simon and Schuster, 1998.

Mills, Simon, *The Titanic in Pictures,* Buckinghamshire, Eng.: Wordsmith Publications, 1995.

Moving Picture News, "Dorothy Gibson Tells Her Story of the *Titanic* Wreck to Our Roving Commissioner," April 27, 1912, p. 7.

The Moving Picture World, "Saved From the *Titanic*," May 11, 1912, p. 539.

New York Dramatic Mirror, "Saved From the *Titanic*: Dorothy Gibson," April 24, 1912, p. 26.

New York Morning Telegraph. "Motion Picture Actress Tells of *Titanic* Wreck," April 21, 1912, p. 2.

New York Telegraph, "Miss Dorothy Gibson Tells of Her Rescue," April 20, 1912.

New York Times, "Some Who Were Saved When the *Titanic* Went Down," April 17, 1912, p. 1.

Parsons, Chauncey L., "Dorothy Gibson From the *Titanic*: An Account of the Shipwreck According to an Actress Who Went Through it," *New York Dramatic Mirror,* May 1, 1912, p. 13.

"Picture Actress Was *Titanic* Wreck Survivor," unidentified, April 27, 1912, Marsha Buckley Collection.

FINDING DOROTHY

Tibballs, Geoff, *The Titanic: The Extraordinary Story of the Unsinkable Ship*, Pleasantville, NY: Readers' Digest, 1997.

Dorothy Gibson Brulatour
Billboard, "Dorothy Gibson," December 2, 1911.
_____. "Dorothy Gibson: The Harrison Fisher Girl with the New American Éclair Stock Co.," November 11, 1911, p. 14.
_____. "The Easter Bonnet," April 20,1912, p. 52-53.
_____. "Leading Moving Picture Actors," December 9, 1911, p. 28.
_____. "Love Finds a Way," January 20, 1912, p. 39.
_____. "A Lucky Holdup," April 6, 1912, p. 29.
_____. "Members of the Éclair Stock Company," February 3, 1912, p. 4.
_____. "Miss Masquerader," November 25, 1911, p. 40.
"Dorothy Gibson Leaves for Europe," unidentified, undated (ca. March 1912)), Marsha Buckley Collection.
Gowan, Phillip and Meister, Brian, "The Saga of the Gibson Women," The *Atlantic Daily Bulletin* , 2002 (Vol. 3), pp. 10-13.
"Miss Dorothy Gibson, Harrison Fisher Muse, Now Picture Star," unidentified, undated (ca. 1911), Marsha Buckley Collection.
Moving Picture News, "Dorothy Gibson," November 18, 1911, p. 8.
_____. "Hands Across the Sea in '76," November 18, 1911, p. 30.
_____. "It Pays to be Kind," March 3, 1912.
_____. "The Kodak Contest," March 3, 1912.
_____. "Loves Finds a Way," January 13, 1912.
_____."Miss Masquerader," November 18, 1911.
The Moving Picture World, "The Awakening," February 10, 1912.
_____. "The Kodak Contest," March 23, 1912.
_____. "Miss Dorothy Gibson," April 27, 1912, p. 344.
_____. "Miss Masquerader," December 9, 1911.
_____. "A New Star in the Picture Firmament," December 2, 1911, p. 720.
_____. "The Revenge of the Silk Masks," May 18, 1912, p. 608, 629.
Naylor, Hazel Simpson, "Some Moving Picture Actors of Note," *American Sunday Monthly Magazine/Chicago Examiner*, undated (ca. January 1912), Marsha Buckley Collection.
New York Courier, "Fisher Girl Joins Éclair," undated (Marsha Buckley Collection).
New York Dramatic Mirror, "The Awakening," February 14, 1912, p. 33.
_____. "Brooms and Dustpans," April 3, 1912, p. 32.
_____. "Dorothy Gibson, A Leading Lady of the Éclair (American) Stock," December 6, 1911, p. 28.
_____. "Dorothy Gibson: Charming Leading Lady with Éclair American Company," January 31, 1912, p. 52.
_____. "Dorothy Gibson: Recently Engaged Leading Lady With the Éclair (American) Company," August 9, 1911, p. 20.
_____. "Éclair Releases," May 15, 1912, p. 27.

BIBLIOGRAPHY

_____. "Gossip of the Studios," August 9, 1911, p. 21.

_____."Hands Across the Sea," November 29, 1911, p. 29.

_____. "The Kodak Contest," March 20, 1912.

_____. "A Living Memory," April 3, 1912.

_____. "Love Finds a Way," January 31, 1911, p. 66.

_____. "A Lucky Holdup," April 17, 1912, p. 31.

_____. "Miss Masquerader," December 6, 1911, p. 34.

_____. "The Musician's Daughter," December 20, 1911, p. 34.

_____. "Personalities of Players," February 28, 1912, p. 30.

New York Morning Telegraph, "Dorothy Gibson: The Popular Leading Lady of the Eclair Films," December 17, 1911.

New York Times, "Auto Suit is Settled," May 22, 1913, p. 2.

_____. "Mrs. Dorothy Brulatour (Obituary), February 21, 1946.

_____. "Mystery in $50,000 Suit," May 5, 1920, p. 22.

_____. "Refuses $48,000 Alimony," August 21, 1919, p. 9.

_____. "Wants Her Income Assured," April 23, 1915, p. 19.

"Photoplay Actress Was Fisher Model," September 11, 1911, unidentified, Marsha Buckley Collection.

"Picture Star Given Reception at Weber's," unidentified, undated (ca. January 1912), Marsha Buckley Collection.

St. Johns, Adela Rogers, "Yesterday's Stars Today: Dorothy Brulatour," May 16, 1934, unidentified, Marsha Buckley Collection.

The Paris Herald, "Miss Fannie Ward and Friends Give 'Movie' Party," December 12, 1924.

People Magazine, "Dorothy Gibson: The silent film star dressed for disaster," March 16, 1998, p. 50.

New York Public Library for the Performing Arts, Billy Rose Theatre Division, Robinson Locke Scrapbooks, Series 3, Vol. 407, pp. 99-102.

Town Topics, "Miss Gibson's Pretty Place," undated (ca.1916), Marsha Buckley Collection.

Fiction

Loos, Anita, *Gentlemen Prefer Blondes,* New York: Boni and Liveright, 1925.

Montanelli, Indro, *General Della Rovere,* New York: Doubleday, 1961.

Film

Citizen Kane (RKO Pictures, 1941). Directed by Orson Welles. Cast: Orson Welles, Dorothy Comingore, Ruth Warwick, Agnes Moorehead. Distributed by Warner Home Entertainment.

General Della Rovere (ZebraFilms/Gaumont, 1959). Directed by Roberto Rossellini. Cast: Vittorio di Sica, Hannes Messemer, Anne Vernon. Distributed by FilmAffinity, Inc.

The Lucky Holdup. Directed by Etienne Arnaud. (Éclair-America Film Company, 1912). Cast: Dorothy Gibson, Lamar Johnstone. Archived at the Library of Congress.

www.ingramcontent.com/pod-product-compliance
Lightning Source LLC
Chambersburg PA
CBHW030417100426

42812CB00028B/2995/J